Traces on the Landscape

Traces on the Landscape

Kent Midgett

Edited and with a foreword
by Douglas Midgett

Mid-Prairie Books

Parkersburg, IA

Copyright © by Mid-Prairie Books, 1998
All rights reserved
Manufactured in the United States of America

Cover Art: Photo of painting by Olive Midgett Kniseley

ISBN 0-931209-80-3

Mid-Prairie Books
P.O. Box 680
Parkersburg, IA 50665
319-346-2048

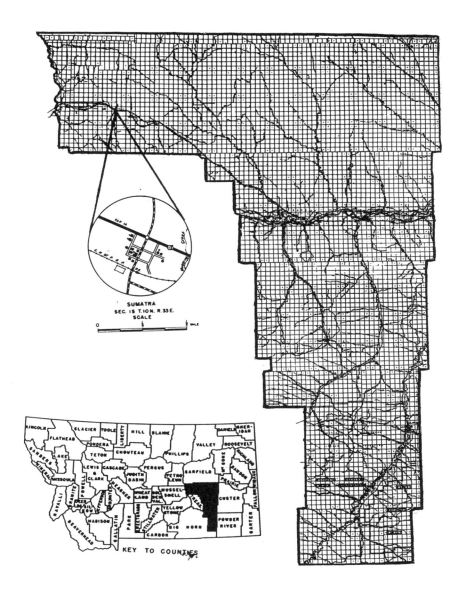

Rosebud County, Montana

SUMATRA

1-Depot
2-RC Church
3-Dormitory
4-School
5-Elevator
6-Hotels
7-General stores
8-Lumber yards
9-Bank
10-Livery stables
11-Drug store
12-Saloon
13-Garage
14-Water Tower

C. M. St.P & Pac RR

Foreword: In the Name of Progress

How does one know in his bones what this continent has meant to Western man unless he has, though briefly and in the midst of failure, belatedly and in the wrong place, made trails and paths on an untouched country and built human living places, however transitory, at the edge of a field he helped break from prairie sod?

Wallace Stegner

In the second decade of this century my grandfather and thousands like him homesteaded or bought land, settled and went about making a garden of the eastern Montana high plains. It seems clear that they possessed equal measures of hope and ignorance of what lay before them. Likewise, my father, when he undertook in the early 1970s to write about his family's experience in that difficult country, had only an inkling of the task he had set upon. It consumed a good part of the rest of his life and what is contained in this volume is most of what he wanted to say.

If he was unprepared for what he witnessed that day in 1970 when he came in sight of the meager remains of Sumatra, so was I unprepared for his account when I undertook to edit and prepare it for publication. Reading it through for the first time I could not help recalling Wallace Stegner's magnificent story of a similar, but distinctly different place in *Wolf Willow*. I don't know if my father ever read Stegner's book. If he didn't, it is probably well, for his task would have seemed even more daunting. If he did and proceeded undaunted, good for him.

Constructing this foreword involved me more in the subject than I might have imagined. It took me in 1997 back to the Sumatra/Hibbard area, and the small neighboring locations of Ingomar and Vananda. I met people, now in their seventies, whose births my grandfather attended. Library work took me from my university at Iowa to my alma mater, the University of Montana, in Missoula. The list of folks who earned my father's thanks in his preface is thus extended to those who helped me.

*   *   *   *

This book is about three things. It is first about my father's family and their experiences in Montana. In that respect it is personal and limited in scope. The experience of numerous others may be reflected in this account of their lives, but my father was under no illusions that his family was typical.

Second, this is a story about a nascent town and its struggles to break free of the constraints that frustrated the ambitions of hundreds like it to amount to something. In this, the story is one of ultimate failure, for Sumatra was eventually not viable. The story is also about community—a real community with people doing things and being actual. These were people who, brought together by some common hopes and ambitions, had to construct community, something beyond a collectivity of individuals. That they did so is testified to by the recurrence of regional reunions that in recent years have drawn hundreds from all parts of the U.S.

The third focus of the book is on people and society. I think this is not something my father attempted with the intention he vested in the other topics, but the sociological portrait of a people encountering a set of circumstances at a specific time in this century is revealed in his writing. I shall elaborate on these themes, but first I must discuss how this all came about—what brought the people to this place. And "the people" includes my father's family.

*   *   *   *

The settling of that arid unpromising stretch of Montana was the culmination of a number of errors of judgment. First, of course, but least blameworthy, were the settlers, themselves. In the first half of the 1910-1920 decade they were subject to a number of lures, all attractive. The Milwaukee Road promoted heavily the region of its recent transcontinental expansion. In particular, the railroad promoters blanketed the midwest with promotional literature. Beginning in 1910 they issued brochures trumpeting the possibilities for settlers interested in Montana. The first of these included a section on "Dry Farming," a term "used to describe those wonderful methods" that promised exceptional crop yields in areas where annual rainfall averaged from 10 to 18 inches.[1] A mention of Montana weather encourages the prospective migrant that "there are few days during the entire year in which outdoor work cannot be done in comfort."[2]

The 1910 brochure specifically mentions the area south of the Musselshell River as one where "some of the best open land open to homestead entry may be found."[3] The railroad also issued a free publication, "Government Homesteads and How to Secure Them." A few years later brochures specific to Eastern Montana (1913) and Musselshell County (1913) were distributed. The text of the 1915 Montana promotion, subtitled "The Treasure State," touted the last four years of development, including prize-winning yields and crop examples from the state.

But perhaps the most dramatic piece of Milwaukee Road promotion is the cover of the 1912 brochure, reproduced on subsequent advertising. A farmer behind a plow and a brace of horses is plowing into the eastern section of a map of Montana. Instead of sod the plow is turning over gold coins. No accompanying text is needed.

The railroad's motivation was obvious. Having completed a rail line through largely unoccupied territory, it would depend on a growing population of consumers and producers. The area could hardly become profitable for the railroad if there was nothing to ship in or out. The railroad's effort was augmented by other promoters—chambers of commerce, land speculators, governmental agencies eager to sell state-owned lands and local boosters in dozens of towns imagining themselves as future Chicagos.

---

[1] Chicago, Milwaukee, and St. Paul Railway Co. (C,M,&St.P), "Montana," (1910), p. 31.

[2] Ibid, p. 4.

[3] Ibid., p. 16.

A second incentive for settlers was the Revised Homestead Act of 1909 which doubled the size of the original grants to 320 acres (a half section). Although the reasoning was dubious, justification for the revision rested on the presumed need for more acreage in dry country. The revision was also predicated on the third incentive, the notion that the problem of aridity could be overcome by instituting a "scientific" planting and plowing regime designed to mitigate the effects of low annual precipitation. This method of dryland farming, championed most vigorously by Hardy Webster Campbell, a South Dakota farmer, required that land lie fallow—but not planted in alternative crops or grasses—every other year. Hence, the need for an allotment of land double the original homestead allocation.

Thus, for the prospective migrant the whole package was there. The railhead was established that would bring goods to the settler and link him to markets for his produce. Land was available to homestead, and when usable homesteads were filed, it could be bought from the Northern Pacific Railroad's allotment or from the state. A method of farming had been developed that claimed to work in dry regions regardless of crop choice.

And for those like my grandfather, who had a chance to visit in advance of a move, they saw it all in action during the 1910-1915 years—abundant precipitation, good crops, a country filling up, the promise of continued prosperity. But they did not know of cycles of wet and dry in this land and what these would mean for their fondest plans.

The second error of judgment—and here we may fault its proponents—was the proposition that there had been developed a foolproof method for farming the dry high plains with nothing but available precipitation. It was really a variation on an older idea, given a new look and scientific imprimatur by Campbell and its other advocates. As early as the 1860s there was a notion that not only could dry regions be farmed without additional water inputs, but that farming would ultimately mitigate that very dryness—"rain follows the plow." As Joni Kinsey suggests, although this idea was "eagerly accepted at first,...today (it) seems so bizarre as to have been a conspiracy concocted solely for capitalist gain, with little regard for the land itself or for those who would make it their home."[4]

Toward the end of the 19th century the scientific version made its appearance in what was termed the "Campbell Method," named for its developer and most enthusiastic promoter. Campbell had developed his approach in South Dakota and found ready acceptance especially on the part of the railroads, eager in their own promotion of the areas opened up by their western extension. The formation of the Campbell System Farming Association—later the Dry Farming Congress—led to annual conferences in western plains cities in Canada and the U.S. These were promotional events, bankrolled by "railroads, bankers, chambers of commerce, state publicity departments, and real estate brokers."[5]

The bottom line is simply that the system did not work. When the wet years of the early teens turned to searing aridity in 1918 and subsequent years no plowing regime could conserve moisture that refused to fall. And some of the practices advocated by the new methodology—deep plowing, summer fallow, "dust mulch"—proved increasingly destructive when drought and wind prevailed. Nonetheless dryland farming methodology was a bill of goods that many were eager to buy—the railroads and boosters seeking to settle the land, national legislators with Jeffersonian notions of empires in the West who passed the Revised Homestead Act, and the prospective farmers for whom it fueled their dreams of acres of waving grain.

The third judgment error was on the part of the Milwaukee Road. In their rush to compete with the Great Northern and the Northern Pacific who had completed their links from Chicago to the west coast, the railroad chose a route of which James Vance notes:

> The construction across the Great Plains was notable mostly for the absence of settlement along the line chosen. In seeking new territory to develop, the Mil-

---

[4] Joni Kinsey, *Plain Pictures: Images of the American Prairie* (Washington: Smithsonian Institution Press, 1996), p. 89.

[5] H. Ross Toole, *Twentieth Century Montana: A State of Extremes* (Norman, OK: University of Oklahoma Press), p. 41.

waukee's locating engineers had certainly found virgin ground. Only later was it to realize how sterile much of it would remain. A casual reading of the timetable for this route is an introduction to the thinness of settlement in the northern Great Plains. Names of obscurity follow one another for most of the seven hundred miles (from Mobridge SD) to Butte.[6]

He goes on to describe the westward extension as "a striking case of a misappraisal of the market."[7] In part this may be 20-20 hindsight, but it is true that the railroad eventually became bankrupt, and although parts of its right-of-way were sold off, track through most of Montana—1055 miles in 1920—has been abandoned and torn up.

In the end, of course, Sumatra would never have existed and the settlement of that region of northwestern Rosebud County would never have been so extensive had not the railroad pushed through the area in 1909. It was truly a case of "If you build it (and promote it heavily), they will come." The sad story was that no one could know just how few could stay.

Family

My father was never under any illusions that his family was typical of the settlers who landed in eastern Montana after 1909. One need only read of the contents of the Midgetts' immigrant car to be aware of the material abundance they possessed relative to many of their neighbors. In addition they brought along two people who served almost as family retainers. Blanche Delaney and Billy Cook were invaluable household residents during the first year in Montana, and although their labor contributed substantially to the family enterprise, their upkeep was largely my grandfather's responsibility.

He was, of course, a professional man, a medical doctor who had already established a successful practice in Illinois when he

---

[6] James Vance, *The North American Railroad: Its Origin, Evolution, and Geography* (Baltimore: The Johns Hopkins University Press, 1995), p. 217.

[7] Ibid., p. 219.

decided upon the Montana move. He brought
in the area, and a substantial (for the time) ba
He had a house constructed for his family
section of farmland with a view to develop
buildings. He later built a house on the farm ar
the latter a two-story affair that was one o
They never lived in tarpaper shacks or sod houses that were home for
many others. He also became a small businessman, operating the
town's drug store.

My grandfather's position as a professional, educated man
and businessman did not go unnoticed by the townspeople and he
became a civic leader in both church and secular affairs. Likewise my
grandmother occupied corresponding positions in roles reserved for
women. If there was anything like a gentry in that little town, they
and a few other similarly placed people—merchants, the banker,
teachers, managers—were it. Sumatra was hardly class-stratified
but there were some whose social positions were special.

A second feature of the family is that, apart from brief
residences on the farm, they were town folk. My father and his
siblings grew up as town kids. He may have spent a few summers
doing farm work but their experiences were much more described by
the town and its diversions, however simple. My Aunt Olive wrote of
this: "I'm sure the struggle was pretty grim for the grownups but for
the kids it was a good place to grow up. The pleasures were simple but
we thought we had everything." She continues, drawing the distinction between town and country: "One of the greatest pleasures we 'city'
kids had was going home with farm families when they came in for
supplies." The contrast is clear. Farm life was an occasional diversion for town children; rural children and adults faced every day the
imperatives that farm living imposed on time and energy.

All of this is not to draw absolute distinctions between the
lives of my father's family and those of the area's majority who were
farmers. Both groups had to contend with life in a land where
amenities were few and the daily tasks of existence were arduous and
time-consuming. But in a context where for many the possibilities
were circumscribed by vagaries of weather, insects, and price fluctua-

eyond their control, my father, his siblings, and some of the
town children had a wealth of opportunities.

Two instances illustrate this. My father's entry into college in
1920 seems to have been foreordained. There was little doubt but that
his direction lay in some vocation that would require a college
education and would necessarily take him away from Sumatra,
probably for good. Thus, whatever had been good and formative
about adolescent years spent in the town, it was not promising enough
to warrant a return. The second event is the family's departure in
1926. Significantly, my grandparents were able to make the move to
Bridger with a clean slate, having sold out their land holdings and
liquidated debts in order to reestablish in their new home. Life may
have become increasingly difficult during their last Sumatra years
when patients could not afford a doctor's services and the farm could
not make money, but they did not have to leave an abandoned farm-
stead with only the sparest of belongings and no prospects in the next
place. One former resident, writing of this time states, "It was no
disgrace to be broke in those days as most everybody was in the same
boat." My grandparents might have been in that boat, but their
heads remained well above water.

Town and Community

To describe Sumatra we can refer to a piece titled "The Plains
Country Town," which appeared in a collected volume in 1979.[8]
Sumatra was an "elevator town," a "T-town," a "railroad town."
That is, it was a "first link between a staple-exporting region and a
world market."[9] It owed its existence and location to the construction
of a railroad through that part of Montana in the first decade of this
century. Its design was platted by the railroad company on a simple
pattern common to western plains towns. The design focuses on the
railroad, with most of the town lying on one side of the tracks and a

---

[8] John C. Hudson, "The Plains Country Town," in *The Great Plains: Environment and Culture,* eds. Brian W. Blout and Frederick C. Luebke (Lincoln, NE: University of Nebraska Press, 1979), pp. 99-118.

[9] Ibid., p. 99.

main street—in Sumatra, "Main Street"—running near perpendicular to the railroad with principal business houses on both sides of the street.

As the region's population grew Sumatra assumed more of what geographers call central place functions. At the outset, aside from the rail station, some of these were demanded almost before there was a town. The promoters, too, recognized the importance of developing such functions for the viability of the new town. In the 1913 Milwaukee Road brochure, "Eastern Montana," Sumatra is described as a "thriving young town" where "nearly all classes of business are represented," but where "there is a good opening for a first-class general store, a drug store, hardware and implement store, and elevator."[10]

One of the first businesses needed was a lumber and coal yard in this treeless region that had no natural fuel. A general store and grain elevator were established by 1911 and the first of two hotels was built the same year. By the time my father's family moved to Sumatra in 1916 the town had another hotel, two more general stores, livery stables, a blacksmith shop that was transforming into an auto garage, another lumber yard, and a saloon. A school had been established in a building that served as the town hall and meeting place for Protestant services. The Catholic Church was in operation and a new depot had replaced the boxcar that originally served.

A cluster of houses completed the town. These were mostly occupied by families who were attached in some way to the commercial, productive and service functions located in the town. It is also likely that some rural families maintained a town house for occupation during the winter, especially after the new school was built in 1916. Thus, the population of town dwellers fluctuated through the year corresponding to the agricultural cycle.

As important as these central place functions were, the activity that drove the whole system was agricultural production. Like most of eastern Montana which had attracted tens of thousands

---

[10] C,M,&St.P, "Eastern Montana," (1913), p. 14.

of rural settlers after 1909, Rosebud County became a grower of grains destined for a national market—an integral, if remote, appendage of agrarian capitalism. In this respect it was economically like any number of colonial locations which grew up during the heyday of mercantile capitalism. Its little towns served as local points of capital accumulation for a vast and growing system. While they were able to generate profit for that system they thrived on its periphery; when they were no longer able to produce efficiently, the system had no use for them. Toole states this dramatically: "These towns were not created for diversion but for cold, hard utility—granary, general store, bank, and church; hot dusty, flat, and gray."[11]

In Sumatra's case I would argue that the town survived longer than it might have, given its declining agricultural fortunes and dwindling rural population, because of the importance of one central place institution: its school. The construction of the school in 1916 and the dormitory in 1920 geographically expanded the influence of the town even as other factors were reducing it. When the school burned in 1964 it really marked the final blow. With only 22 students left in the school, the remaining families could not see the viability of a rebuilt institution and the town soon became the ghost we see today.

Despite this history, the grim picture painted by Toole, while not essentially wrong, does not adequately capture the experience of northwestern Rosebud County and much of the rural and small town West. If we are to make sense of the human landscape that emerged we must go beyond utility and characterizations that account for the settlements as they were generated by capitalist expansion and individual greed. We must examine what was formed as community, the human aggregations, people who came to live in the same place, most drawn by similar motives and ambitions, whose lives became intertwined in multiple ways.

In many of his writings Wallace Stegner gives the lie to the myth of the rugged individualist as exemplar of the western tradition. He demonstrates with great clarity that the individual, isolated and facing the harsh life on an undeveloped land, could

---

[11] Toole, p. 65.

hardly survive, let alone prosper. Rather, the success of human settlements however brief, was possible only through the mutual assistance and recognition of common purpose that we call community. People assisted one another, took responsibility for their neighbors' welfare, exchanged labor, eased the accommodation of newcomers, and created a collective sense of identity that lingers long after the demise of the physical town.

Three examples of this sense of community will suffice. Former residents and their children continue to return to Sumatra, Ingomar and Vananda, and retain an abiding interest in these places. "Tri-City" reunions in 1976 and 1996 drew many hundreds to the area even though the towns had mostly disappeared.[12] A second example is the sentiment given voice by a life-long resident born in the Sumatra area in 1927. As we discussed the past, brief heyday of the town he remarked, "Boy you should have seen this place then. There was a real community here."

Finally, there is evidenced a commonplace feature of community identity—the opposition to other towns. A woman explained her and her husband's desire to resettle in the rural Sumatra area as opposed to Ingomar: "People here are so nice to each other; they get along. They aren't like that in Ingomar." The truth or falsity of such statements is irrelevant. The importance, clear to anyone who has ever attended a small-town high school basketball game between rival neighbors, is that "we" are special, and that quality derives from our conception of our collective selves.

People and Society

If we are to put the experiences of my father and his family in context we need to examine a few more issues on which this book touches but only occasionally elaborates. We need to construct a portrait of the people who came to inhabit this place, their origins both geographical and ethnic, and the pattern of migration that brought them to Montana. We need to know something about their

---

[12] Ingomar continues to have a resident population and an important gathering spot, the Jersey Lilly, a bar/restaurant/dance hall of some renown.

occupational backgrounds and the skills they brought. We must also look at the larger social formation in which this activity took place—the forces that shaped the occupation of the Northern Plains and subsequently depopulated the region.

The people who settled in northwestern Rosebud County came mostly from the U.S. Upper Midwest. This was the area targeted by promotional literature distributed by the Milwaukee Road and other boosters. The Midwest was also an area that, by 1910, was filled up in that opportunities for land acquisition had ceased. In 1910 a large percentage of the American population was involved directly in agriculture and in states like Iowa and Illinois there were few opportunities left for those who wanted to commence or expand farming.

The opening of homesteads in Montana coupled with the enlargement of the allotment seemed to be the chance many were seeking. Family histories reveal numerous moves from Iowa, Minnesota, Illinois, Indiana, and the eastern portions of the Dakotas and Nebraska. Many of these were first generation European immigrants who were making another move in their journeys across America. A somewhat larger number had been established for a generation or more, but were likewise in search of new lives.

The migration pattern is curious in that, apart from links that brought some family members, usually siblings, to the Rosebud region, there is nothing like the "chain" migrations that resulted in large numbers of immigrants from the same origin arriving at the same destination. The creation of ethnic colonies of immigrants from various European origins was commonplace in the Upper Midwest where many of these communities retain a flavor of their ethnic origins, but this was a rarity in eastern Montana.

I suggest that a primary reason such colonization and ethnic community formation did not occur relates to the rapidity with which the Northern Plains population grew. From 194,000 in 1900 the region, which includes eastern Montana, increased to 620,000 people in 1920.[13]

---

[13] Mary W. M. Hargreaves, *Dry Farming in the Northern Great Plains: Years of Readjustment, 1920-1990* (Lawrence, KN: University Press of Kansas, 1993), p. 4.

Toole notes that by 1909, just after the revisions in the Act, the Miles City Land Office was processing 1200 homestead filings per month, a figure comparable to other offices east of the divide in Montana.[14] The rush for free land or relatively cheap land following the "honyocker" surge precluded the possibility of widespread growth of ethnic communities.[15] It was also a movement abbreviated by the subsequent failure of many of these enterprises. Hargreaves states that, "One scholar has estimated that as many as three-fourths of the people who homesteaded Montana between 1909 and 1918 left their holdings by 1922."[16]

Although their European origins were diverse, the settlers in Rosebud County displayed some common characteristics. Few were professionally trained or highly educated (J.E. and Amy Midgett were exceptions), and most came from working class or agrarian backgrounds. As in much of the newly settled West many embarked on a farming existence without much experience. Most were young, just starting adult careers or with nascent families. Most had young children or were soon to have them, adding to the burdens imposed by this harsh land. And because they were young and because many had traveled to Montana leaving extended family behind, they had limited family-based support systems. They would need to depend on neighbors, only recently strangers, and on the forging of community.

Where did these people, this experience fit into a larger society undergoing rapid and often disruptive change? They constituted the last significant movement of people to the West, filling in some of the vast spaces opened up by the destruction of the Plains Indian cultures and societies and the closing of the open range. Turner and the U.S. Census Bureau may have declared the frontier closed some decades before but it was not until the decade of the teens that some very empty spaces were filled in.

---

[14] Toole, p. 59.

[15] The process of chain migrations leading to ethnic community formation simply takes longer, since early settlers establish, send for relatives and friends, who in turn follow the same pattern.

[16] Hargreaves, p. 4.

So the settlers came to Rosebud County and created farmsteads and small towns and many were gone within a decade. The population figures in Table I do not quite indicate how precipitous was this decline, for by the time of the 1920 census many families had given up and many young men who had been in the Army during World War I had not returned to Montana.

Table I
Northwest Rosebud County Population

District	1920	1930	1940
Bascom	140	130	52
Hibbard	100	72	16
Sumatra	415	338	151
Ingomar	416	312	153
Vananda	371	285	184
Gorath/Elmer	34	53	21
Total	1476	1190	577

We may attribute the demise of towns and community life in the Sumatra-Ingomar-Vananda area to vicissitudes of weather and insect pests, and we may say that the experiment of dryland farming in this region was doomed at the outset. And certainly these are undeniable truths. But it is also true that wealth was generated by the labor of those who settled this area, even if for a relatively short time. And during that time the institutions of a nation's capitalist system likewise appeared in northwest Rosebud County. The railroad linked local farmers and their production to markets national and international; it connected them with suppliers of goods they required or desired; banks were established in each of the three towns; representatives of larger companies located in the towns. In short, the mechanisms for appropriating wealth produced by the work of these people was well in place.

And once the agricultural boom in the county had passed how were the residents served by these institutions? First we must note that the small towns and rural dwellers were not well served by the public administrations closest to them. Toole notes that the state legislature's 1915 devolvement of control to the counties regarding county subdivision contributed to the formation of 28 new counties between 1910 and 1925.[17] This was entirely in the interest of boosters in prospective county seat towns, but it took place during a period that saw Montana's agricultural fortunes severely impacted and its rural population declining after 1918. The consequence, in the face of drought, insect infestations, and declining prices after 1919, was a vast inflation of administrative costs borne by a decreasing number of residents on impoverished holdings. The outcome was property confiscation in lieu of taxes and heavy involvement of county governments in the land market. Although Rosebud County already existed in 1910, parts of it were subsequently whittled away to make new counties, reducing its property value base and increasing the burden on those who remained.

Rosebud County farmers, because their production was tied to distant market demand, were subject to price fluctuations over which they had no control. During World War I, when incidentally their yields were impressive, they profited in a world where European agriculture was in ruins. Wheat prices rose every year up to 1919, even as the drought was upon them. But the end of the War and the resurgence of European production ended the windfall of the mid-teens. In 1920 the price paid for wheat was more than halved and it continued to decline as European production regained pre-war levels by the mid-twenties.[18]

Another serious blow for many small Montana towns was the failure of their banks during the early twenties. Built in many cases on the shallowest of soil, banks in the state had proliferated during the previous decade as the agricultural and small-town boom had proceeded. Toole refers to the "over-banked" condition that existed by 1920.[19] Dependent almost entirely on local economic factors, many were devastated by the events of the late teens. When more than half failed between 1920 and 1926, the towns and rural areas they

---

[17] Toole, p. 92.

[18] Ibid, p. 90.

[19] Ibid, p. 86. See also Clarence W. Groth, "Sowing and Reaping: Montana Banking, 1910-25," *Montana, the Magazine of Western History* 20(4):28-35, (1970).

served were often without credit facilities during a time of desperate need.

Finally, there was no significant safety net for most of the victims of this devastation. Federal seed programs could not come close to making up shortages in planting material once the drought was in full swing. The growing catastrophe—for that is what it was for many who had to endure it—occurred a decade before the depression and the subsequent social legislation that would provide some relief for those caught in such circumstances. The unfortunates in Rosebud County and elsewhere on the Northern Plains were pretty much left to their own devices, a people cultivated for as long as their labor created profit for others, but largely abandoned once the hard times struck.

*   *   *   *

In *Wolf Willow* Wallace Stegner uses a weaving metaphor to characterize the experience of farming settlers on the high plains: "Failure was woven into the very web of Whitemud. It was the inevitable warp, as hope was the woof, of that belated frontier."[20] The hope, the vision, the imagined garden occluded the fundamental conditions of landscape, weather, isolation that inevitably defeated the purposes of the settlers.

In early summer of 1997 the high plains of Montana were green and lush. A cool, rainy spring and early summer had contributed to the verdant landscape I encountered as I drove west up Highway 212 from the Yellowstone River toward Sumatra. The bottomland south of Vananda was partially flooded by Big Porcupine Creek and even the tableland at the divide around Sumatra was a picture of a fecund prairie. I imagined this country when my grandfather first saw it in 1913, green and growing crops after the few years of abundant moisture that preceded his visit. And I could understand his imagination of a place that would grow like a garden in this stark, open, empty land. He could see the woof; his vision was the hope; the

---

[20] Wallace Stegner, *Wolf Willow* (Lincoln NE: University of Nebraska Press, 1980), p. 255.

warp, the forces that would spell failure for his venture and others', was yet concealed and invisible.

Preface

This is a story of a family, my family, the Midgett family, who moved from the relative comforts of a small town in southeastern Illinois to the rigorous and highly uncertain existence of homesteading days in east central Montana. It is a narrative similar to that of thousands of settlers who came west during the land rush between 1910 and 1920. In this new country, according to the advertising campaigns put on by federal and state governments, the railroads, and the Chambers of Commerce, a man could become wealthy merely by turning over the virgin sod and scratching in a few bushels of grain.

Hundreds and even thousands of these simple folk, like the Midgetts, succumbed to the glowing picture of happiness and prosperity depicted in the colorful ads placed in all the larger newspapers and pasted on billboards, barns and fences all over the eastern and central states. Eastern Montana was the "land of milk and honey" where anyone, whether he knew anything about farming or not, could set himself up on 320 acres of virgin land and within five years find his dream of financial independence come true. The dry land of western Rosebud County in 1910 was a prime example of this terrible hoax.

The story of these venturesome folk has rarely been told. Comparatively few of Montana's contemporary residents realize the hardships under which these remarkable people lived during the first two or three decades of the 1900's. However, with the exception of a few of the hardiest, most of the rural population of this area have left. Millions of acres that were turned into waving fields of golden grain no longer show a trace of the plow. Many of the little towns that sprang up along the Milwaukee Road are now specters on the prairies, their inhabitants either deceased or scattered to the winds.

An example is the little village of Sumatra whose townsmen, at the time of my story, had great aspirations of building it into the trading center of a large territory extending seventy-five miles north and south and twenty-five miles from east to west. From a lively town of more than three hundred residents in 1920 it has gradually dwindled to a single family, the postmistress, her husband and six children, who live in a trailer house close by a second one in which the post office is located.

My father, Joseph Elmer, and his family, my mother, Amy and their five children were a small but important part of this community. It is a story of this family, their activities in the community, their relations and interdependence with the lives of the other hard working people around them and the huge amount of give and take required to live in this frontier land.

My decision to write this story became final after a visit my wife and I made to the area. The idea came to me years earlier while many of the principal characters were still living and much more first hand information might have been available. Even though I hadn't seen Sumatra since 1926 I was convinced there was a story there that should be told.

My regret is that I did not do the job twenty or thirty years ago when my memory of the characters and events of the period was much more vivid. With the help of my parents, especially my mother with her keen retrospection into events even as far back as her own childhood, I am sure much of the local history during this period and the people who made it all happen could have been more fully realized than I am able to do.

For memories of those happenings and the characters who played a part in them I am deeply indebted to many people but especially to my brother, Bob, and sisters, Betty, Olive and Phyllis whose recollections of the period are still quite vivid. Others who have come to my assistance from time to time as the story has progressed are some of the old timers who were contemporaries of the Midgetts during this period. A few such as the John Kluks, Vern Kestersons, Ralph Guthridges, Grandma La Furge and her offspring, schoolmates Gladys Kreider and Elizabeth Hecker, and some of the Zaharkos still reside in the same general area. Although all are much older in years they still retain many memories of those days.

Probably my greatest assistance has come from Ed and Anna Dorothy who still live about twelve miles south of Sumatra in their little farm house that has stood on the same site for over fifty years. Anna, a classmate of my sister Betty, was a brilliant student in high school and she apparently has lost none of her powers of retention of events of the period. Her collection of pictures, newspapers and other mementos together with her memory, has helped me to put the pieces together in a much more orderly fashion than I otherwise could have done.

Others who have made significant contributions are the Clair Ballards, the Paul McDonalds, and the Harold Kickers—the female halves of which were three of the Hayes sisters, Alene, Thelma and Goldie. Additional information secured from a survey questionnaire from about 35 former residents of Sumatra and vicinity not only helped to enhance my recollections but provided me with names of people and places I had forgotten, as with dates and events, many occurring after I and family left the area.

Of these respondents, special thanks go to Helen (Holmes) Messmer, Albert Bender and Ralph Guthridge, for the pages upon pages of information that they took time to compile for me. Having lived in the area almost all but the last four years, Ralph brought me pretty well up to date on the important events that have occurred in and around Sumatra over the last fifty years. Helen's remarkable memory and her ability to put her recollections in writing provided me with scores of incidents of the earlier days that helped to make life worthwhile during those homesteading days from 1910 to 1925. Albert's close contact with the schools in Sumatra and Ingomar, and his continued interest in the old homestead enabled him to describe the gradual deterioration of the area and the ultimate demise of the little town of Sumatra and to supply reliable dates relating to many of the changes that took place during the past half century.

I am also indebted to Alice (Batson) Bircher, the Verne Kestersons, the Ed Dorothys, Alvin Wedemeyer, and Katherine (Midgett) Mitchell for the use of their pictures, annuals, papers, and other recorded sources of valuable information.

Others who took time to return my questionnaire and thereby added much to my collection of facts and figures were George Max Booher, Donald W. Davis, Ethel (Jennings) Hamilton, Louise Hamre, Geneva (Witt) Highland, Mamie (Morton) Jennings, Ralph P. Jones, Marguerite (Cody) Knapp, Helen (Smith) Mays, Ernest A. Richenbach, Jr., Lucian B. Smith, Myrtle (Smith) Stansfield, Lyle and Margie (Betty) Stewart, Josephine (McGlumphy) Vogt, Everett and Marguerite (McQuiston) Welsh, Lloyd Wilson, Marvin Witt, and Helen (Booher) Zamzow. Thank all of you for your help.

Last but not least, my gratitude goes to Mrs. Daniel Clifton, postmistress, who, with her husband and children, have been the only residents of the Sumatra town site for the last eight or ten years. Mrs. Clifton's account of the events of 1967 made it possible for me to conclude my story of the Midgett family and its final connection with Sumatra.

My quest for additional information was made difficult by the lack of a complete file of Sumatra weekly newspapers. After preliminary inquiries at the University of Montana and Montana State University libraries failed to produce a single copy of either the original *Sumatra Record* or its successor, the *Sumatra Sun*, I was a little discouraged. Only four or five issues had turned up over more than a year's time and I began to think I was destined to depend entirely on my own memory and the information that I had been able to compile from the returned questionnaires.

Imagine my delight when in May of 1975, while attending a conference in Helena, I was informed by Mrs. Harriett Meloy, librarian at the Montana State Historical Society, that issues of the *Sumatra Sun* from early in 1922 to its demise late in 1925 had been recorded on film and were available on loan through the University of Montana Library. Many hours of viewing the microfilm of Sumatra happenings rewarded me with many pages of information regarding people, places, and events I would not have been able to secure in any other way.

Since this is a story of a relatively short period in the lives of but a single family I have made no attempt to document all the facts and figures presented by references to source information or printed records of the times and places mentioned. I have tried to keep it as simple as possible, yet as factual and complete as the available information would permit. My only purpose in putting this story together is to give its readers as accurate a picture as I can of the way one family lived and reacted to the hardships and pleasures of a rather rough era in Montana history.

In this account there are no mysteries to unravel, no murders to solve, and not even a heavy love affair to make the heart flutter a little from time to time. Still I believe this story is worth recounting because it tells of the daily lives of an ordinary family and its friends and neighbors. What could a person write about that would be more important and interesting than a story of people trying to cope with the task of living under very difficult and discouraging conditions?

Missoula, Montana, 1976

Chapter I

Late spring is probably the most beautiful season of the year in eastern Montana. With the melting of the winter snows and arrival of welcome, though sparse, spring rains the country is as verdant as it ever will be. Sagebrush, extending in all directions as far as the eye can see, changes from its winter gray to a tinge of light green. The undergrowths of spiny cactus begin to show their exquisite blooms of gold and purple. Thousands of clumps of bunch grass try to thrust their fuzzy heads above the heavy gumbo that holds them captive. On this mid-morning in May the rays of a bright sun turn myriad droplets of water from last night's rain into countless diamonds sparkling across the landscape.

"I don't know just what I expect to see." My wife, Adelaine, does not reply as we approach the top of the low divide that separates the small streams flowing westward to the Musselshell and the Missouri from those flowing east and southward toward the Yellowstone River. Traveling east on Montana Highway 12 in the no man's land of sagebrush, cactus, prairie dogs, jack rabbits, and rattlesnakes in northwestern Rosebud County, we are about midway between the two towns of Roundup and Forsyth. We passed the last semblance of habitation about fifteen miles back at Melstone, a freight division point on the Milwaukee Railroad. The places where the embryo hamlets, Bascom and Hibbard, had once shown signs of developing into viable little country towns are now only bare spots in the prairie a mile or more off the highway.

Adelaine has never been through this part of Montana except by night train. Sitting beside me, she cannot guess what lies ahead as we top the ridge and look anxiously toward the horizon three miles away. She says nothing and I am left to my own reflections on what was, and I believe I hope still will be, the lively little town that I knew so well more than fifty years ago. Perhaps I should know better, as I have heard from various sources that Sumatra has changed and I might be greatly disappointed by what I will see. Perhaps that is why my curiosity has never been strong enough to take me back to see the place where I and the rest of the Midgett clan spent ten hard but happy years. Even though Adelaine and I lived in Harlowton in the thirties, only a hundred miles from Sumatra, and often drove through Roundup on the north-south Highway 87, only fifty miles away, we never took that extra hour or two to satisfy any curiosity I may have had.

Now it is May 1970. We left our home in Missoula three days ago for a week's vacation traveling around the state of Montana and seeing some attractions we might have missed on previous trips. After visiting a couple of days with our son, Bruce, and his family in Havre we spent most of Sunday examining and taking pictures of the ghost towns of Kendall and Maiden, a few miles north of Lewistown, before driving on to Roundup to stay overnight.

For some reason I can't explain, we decided before we left home to take the fifty mile detour to Sumatra before going on to Billings and Yellowstone Park. And here we are, three short miles from our objective. But we cannot realize that what we are to see is no longer Sumatra but only its ghost, a mere skeleton of what it had been during the years of the Midgett family's residence over a half century ago.

It is the Sumatra of 1970, not 1920, that appears in the distance as we crest the hill and drive on toward our destination. Our first view from a mile or two away is prophetic of things to come. On the far horizon one of the few remaining structures is superimposed upon and completely framed by the outline of a second and larger building beyond it. From its general shape and the cross on top, I can identify the nearer building as the Catholic Church. For a moment I do not recognize the further one—then suddenly I know. It is the big white house my father built in 1916 on the hill on the east edge of town.

Such a spectacle could not have occurred when Sumatra was the village of my memory. Forty or fifty structures of various sizes and shapes had lined the eight or ten streets that ran through the little town in 1920. Some of them would have obstructed the line of vision between the Church and that big house on the hill, but those buildings no longer exist. Nor do any but two or three of the others that I remember so well from the days of my youth.

Main Street, all three blocks of it, cutting the town in two equal parts, remains but the tracks have grown dim and rutted from lack of travel over the past decade or more. It is no longer lined by fifteen or twenty shops and stores in which the town's business was carried on. No longer standing side by side the two three-story frame hotels at the south end of the street near the railroad tracks. Three general stores farther to the north have disappeared with little to show where they once stood. A hole full of broken bricks and rubble marks the site of the town's only bank. Two lumber yards that flourished during the early years of development are gone without a single two-by-four or strand of wire to point out their locations. Even the town's one and only saloon, usually the last survivor of a dying community, has totally disappeared. Across the street, the only trace left of Dad's drug store and office is a shallow hole in the ground where the basement had been. Farther north on the west side of the street where the big store, the garage and the printing office stood there is only empty space. The only building still standing on Main Street is a stranger to me. I later learn it was Tom Brown's garage, built of cement blocks sometime in the late twenties or early thirties. Its lone presence adds to the sadness of the occasion.

As we search for other landmarks I might recognize, a feeling of great sadness comes over me. No visible sign indicates where the big railroad depot and warehouse had been. Two grain elevators and coal sheds on the south side of the tracks have vanished as have the railroad section house and water tank that supplied the big steam locomotives that pulled the hundred car freight trains and six daily passenger trains that served the little towns along the Milwaukee Road. The passenger trains are gone and the few remaining people in the area no longer have any regular transportation service. All that remains of the once busy village are two or three pens, and the chute of the large stockyard from which thousands of cattle and sheep were shipped in better times.

Approaching the town from the west I noticed the school buildings that I, my brother Bob, and two sisters, Betty (known as

Elizabeth in those days) and Olive, attended for the better part of ten years, have completely vanished. In fact, the coup-de-grace for the town itself occurred on the cold winter night of December 17, 1964, when the last of five school buildings was totally destroyed by fire. The whole school, both grade and high, had been moved into the dormitory in the forties when the student body had dwindled to the point where it was financially impossible to continue operating more than one building. With that building gone, and no prospects of an increase in population, the district tax base was no longer able to provide and support a new school for the few remaining children. Most of those left now go to school at Ingomar, twelve miles to the east, or Melstone, seventeen miles west.

All the other streets are completely obliterated, their tracks washed out and overgrown by the sparse vegetation that grows in this arid climate. Except for the few remnants of buildings still standing a stranger passing through might believe the area to be virgin land once occupied by one or two families. Other than the two buildings that form the picture we saw as we first approached the town only three habitable structures remain, the cement garage on the east side of the Main Street and two small mobile homes. One of the latter houses the postmistress and her family and the other serves as the post office and a little store with a single gas pump. The four or five other structures in sight are only broken down shacks in which horses and cattle shelter from the blazing summer sun and the raging winter blizzards.

Such is the picture of a ghost town we did not expect to find, a ghost town _not_ included in the annals of early day Montana history, a ghost town whose environs _did not_ produce millions of dollars in gold and silver bullion, a ghost town whose population _did not_ grow from half a dozen hungry prospectors to a busy city of ten thousand souls in less than a decade, a ghost town _not_ encircled by great holes and even greater heaps of red earth and slag, a ghost town that _did not_ need a "Committee of Vigilantes" to keep law and order. No, Sumatra was none of these, but it is still the ghost of one of the many little Montana towns whose people had great hopes and aspirations; people who fought a hard but losing battle against nature to make a living for their families; people who refused to give in to the inevitable until driven from their homes and farms by the relentless perennial forces of destructive drought, searing heat, insect infestation, and stifling dust storms; people who made their contributions, great and small, to the development and history of eastern Montana. They left and never came back; but their ghosts are still there for one who remembers.

Chapter II

It was about 10:30 on the cool, drizzly morning of October 12, 1914, when No. 15, the crack Milwaukee Olympian, slowed to a hissing stop. The sign on the side of the little station house indicated we had arrived at Hibbard, Montana. The trip of four and a half weary days in the crowded Pullman sleeper was over at last and my father and mother, two sisters, Kate Elizabeth and Lillian Olive, brother, Robert Lavern and I climbed down the coach's four steps and stretched our legs in the wide open spaces of our new home in eastern Montana.

Although we were glad to arrive at our destination, it was also a little difficult for us to realize we were nearly 2,000 miles away from the two little towns of Flat Rock and Palestine in southeastern Illinois, where my parents and their forebears had made their homes for over half a century.

My parents had been married in a little country church, Wesley Chapel, about halfway between the two towns, on the last day of the week of the last month of the last year of the 19th century, December 31, 1900. After graduating from Illinois Medical College in 1903, my father first hung his shingle in his home town of Flat Rock and in 1909 moved the ten miles to Palestine. I had arrived on the scene a year before he graduated and Elizabeth came along two years later. Robert was born in 1909 and Olive made her appearance in 1912.

The move to Palestine proved to be a wise one and within a year or two my father had established himself as a successful young physician. I am sure any notion of "going west" was far from his thoughts as late as the spring of 1913. He was in his mid-thirties and everything was going his way. There was no apparent reason why he should have made another change of location. Nevertheless, it was then the seed of an idea was planted and began to grow in his mind.

Our minister of the Methodist Church in Palestine, Reverend J. M. Adams, had a brother, Reverend C. P. Adams, who was visiting from Montana. The latter and his family had homesteaded two years earlier, after the Homestead Act of 1909 opened up 320-acre tracts (half sections) of land for settlement in the western part of Rosebud County in east central Montana. The sojourning pastor was a Sunday dinner guest at our home and Montana became the subject of conversation. Dad's interest began to grow. During the next few days other talks took place, mostly centering on the challenge offered to a young physician to serve a clientele of a few hundred hardy pioneer families scattered over more than a thousand square miles of rugged dryland farm and ranch country.

The seed germinated rapidly—perhaps more rapidly than even Dad intended. Completely sold on Montana after his excellent crop in 1912, Reverend Adams was very convincing in his picture of the possibilities of production in this virgin land. Raised on a farm, Dad had stayed close to the soil, growing a prolific garden every summer. I believe he had always entertained the possibility of some day returning to the farm. Maybe now was the time. The next few evenings were devoted to some very serious family discussions of the situation and by Friday a decision was made. Dad would go to Montana with Reverend Adams when he returned that weekend and would spend ten days looking over the situation. He hastily packed his suitcase and Sunday morning the two men boarded the train for Chicago and Montana.

When Dad returned home his enthusiasm had not waned one bit. Apparently nothing he saw during his ten-day visit detracted from the image painted by the good pastor. The late February and early March chinooks had mostly melted the big drifts of winter snow and there was plenty of surface water and subsoil moisture to start the new season. By late April the countryside was already showing promise of a third consecutive good crop year. A picture post card of him in front of a typical homestead shack arrived in June from Mrs. Adams. The news of lots of rain in May and June only hastened the decision which was probably already in its final stages.

As the summer months passed, Dad and Mom talked to many of their numerous kinfolk about the matter but their final decision owed much to a letter they received early in September. It was virtually a petition, written by Reverend Adams and signed by fifteen or twenty of the settlers, most of whom Dad had met during his visit. Most of the crops had been harvested and bumper yields had generally resulted, even on stubbled-in fields growing their second crop of grain. Decision time had arrived and, after another huddle or two, Dad announced in October that the Midgetts would go to Montana in the fall of 1914.

There were many reasons why they chose to wait a year before leaving for the West and an entirely new way of life. Dad was never one to make hasty decisions about anything. In his medical practice he was very painstaking and deliberate in his diagnosis of a case and his decision as to the method of treatment. Even though modern methods and remedies were not available to him, he lost a very small percentage of his patients.

Many factors entered the picture in my parents' final decision. Both of them, well-educated for the times in which they lived, were very ambitious for their children and hoped to give them an opportunity to get a good education. With only single-teacher, eight-grade schools in this new country, and no high school within 50 miles, this matter was a great concern. Dad asked Elizabeth and me what we thought about it. I don't remember our answers but apparently they satisfied him.

My parents were very zealous Methodists, but they apparently had no qualms on that score after meeting and developing the friendship of the Adams family who had already pioneered the way in this new land. The practice of the Christian religion was already well established by these and others in the area. Their faith was never shaken and concerning the move it never seemed to pose a serious problem for my parents.

Another serious consideration for Dad was finding a doctor to replace himself and take over his practice. He could not run out on the people of Palestine and vicinity who had depended on his services for the past four or five years without making sure those services continued to be available to them. Since doctors were at a premium in those days, he needed time to find a capable replacement. It was June of

1914 before a young medical school graduate from the University of Illinois came to work with Dad and decided to take over his practice.

Other problems that required time for their solution involved disposition of the home property and selection and sale of those items we would not take to our new home. Sending out statements and collecting accounts due him for medical services took much of Dad's time during the last three months before leaving. His efforts were well rewarded when, by the middle of September, he had amassed a total of more than $3,000 in cash, with additional promissory notes of over $1,000, which he left with a Palestine bank for collection and deposit to his account.

In the year after the final resolution to go West, a second decision Dad made probably had the most far-reaching effect on our lives during the next ten years. This was his resolve to go back to the farm and his purchase of a section of land (640 acres) adjacent to the Adams place. Yet another reason for the year's delay was to allow sufficient time to choose a location, lay plans, and build a new home that was to be ready for us when we arrived in Montana. Since it was already fall when the final decision to leave was made it was too late to start construction until late spring of 1914.

The day for our departure was finally set for Monday, October 8. The home property on Grand Prairie Street had been sold to a young couple who were moving to Palestine from another state. A public auction sale disposed of most household furnishings, implements, and livestock we had not planned to ship and the rest was passed around among relatives. The new doctor bought most of Dad's office and medical equipment and was already well established in the same location. Arrangements had been made by correspondence with Reverend Adams for the purchase of the land and construction of our new home at Hibbard.

A railroad freight car, known as an immigrant car, which was to carry our remaining possessions over the long distance via the Illinois Central and the Chicago, Milwaukee, and St. Paul and Pacific railroads, was loaded on Wednesday, October 3. Both ends of the car were filled with house and office furnishings, a Model T Ford, and some machinery Dad had decided to keep. After two weeks supply of hay and grain were stowed away, Daisy, the cow, and Cricket, our faithful little bay mare, were led into their stalls in the middle of the car just before the train pulled out early the next morning with Billy Cook, a young friend of Dad's, in charge.

The next few days found the Midgetts spreading themselves around among the relatives, and Dad took advantage of the contacts to do a little selling job on Montana. After attending Sunday school and church, the final Sabbath Day in Palestine was spent packing luggage for the long trip. Mamma was given a lot of help by a friend of the family, Mrs. Blanche Delaney, a widow, who, having no children, had taken a great fancy to my sister, Olive, and had practically raised her from birth. She insisted from the very beginning that she accompany us to Montana, and she had her bags packed when we boarded the train for Chicago about noon on Monday. At last we said good-bye to Palestine and all the friends and relatives who had come to the station to see us off. There must have been a few qualms but I doubt any of us had regrets as the train pulled away from the station and our old friends receded further and further into the distance.

*   *   *   *

Now, four days later we were in Montana, 2,000 miles from our former home but only 200 yards from the home in which we expected to live for many years in the future. It appeared news of our expected arrival had preceded us when, as we stepped down to the platform, we were greeted by a dozen or more of the inhabitants of this sparsely settled frontier community. It was evident these people were not strangers to my father for he had met most of them while visiting here a year and a half earlier. Among those on the welcoming committee were the two Rasque brothers, Moody and Joe, and their dad, Matt, who ran the general store and was the postmaster of the little village. Others who shook hands with Dad were Nels Hamre, the railroad section boss, and his two youngsters, Thelma and Arthur, and D. W. Peyton and son, Howard, who lived about two miles south of the Hibbard town site.

Although Dad's greeting to these people was very cordial, he seemed to sense something was missing. His eyes traveled over the group apparently trying to find the face of the man whose powers of persuasion were responsible for us being here. His apprehension was heightened when, after the train had pulled out, we heard the galloping hooves of a horse with a rider coming across the tracks toward us.

The horseman was Hubert Morris, Mrs. Adams' brother, who pulled up his steed and, after dropping the reins on the ground, rushed up and shook Dad's hand. It was not a happy greeting for his first words were, "I'm sorry to be late getting here but I'm also sorry to report that I have bad news for you. Reverend Adams is seriously ill with double pneumonia and Mrs. Adams is not able to leave her husband to meet you."

Since no one in the area yet owned an automobile, a fast team of horses hitched to a buggy was on its way to pick up Dad and take him to the Adams ranch. Ten minutes later the Reverend's son, Morris, an eleven-year-old, and his sixteen-year-old sister, Argin, drove up. Hubert exchanged places with the two children, Dad picked up the pill bag he always carried, jumped into the rig, and they started the two and a half mile trip to his first patient in Montana. After buying a few groceries, Argin and Morris rode the saddle horse home.

Dad's sudden departure left the rest of us stunned, huddling in the little station house out of the misty rain—but not for long. Our welcoming committee picked up our luggage and led the way across the railroad and south up the main thoroughfare of the two-street hamlet. On the way Joe Rasque informed us that for the next few days we would be quartered in the school house as our new home wasn't yet far enough along to live in. Of course, this was quite a disappointment to my mother but when Mr. Hamre informed us the railroad car, containing our household goods, livestock, and Model T had not yet arrived, it was about the last straw.

Upon arrival at the one-room school house, two blocks up the road, we found we already had many more good friends. As we walked in, five or six women welcomed us to our temporary abode which they had spent the past couple of days cleaning and making habitable. The desks were piled in one corner of the room and curtains hung so it was divided into three or four rooms of very comfortable size.

Because of her husband's illness, Mrs. Adams, the teacher, had been unable to continue in her job for the past two or three days and there had been no school. Since the Rasques, who also were the carpenters, expected to have the house ready in less than a week, and Mrs. Adams would not be able to return to her school during that period, the use of the school house was a Godsend, as there was no place else in Hibbard that could accommodate a group of our size.

By the time we were partially settled and our suitcases unpacked, two or three beds had been set up, a rough dining table and some benches had been brought in, and a few other articles of furniture were scattered among the rooms where they would do the most good. In the northwest corner of the building a large wood and coal heater with a metal jacket around it provided plenty of heat for that time of year. I was given the job of replenishing fuel from the bin attached to the building's west side.

We had all been so busy that none of us realized it was already noontime. In fact my mother's watch showed nearly one P.M. We had been asleep during the night when the train had passed from Central to Mountain time and no one had thought to turn our time pieces back an hour. Mother had not had time to give a thought to what we would have to eat but here again our friends were far ahead of us.

A little after noon Mrs. Jackson and Mrs. Oscar Peyton walked in the door carrying baskets full of food. Fifteen minutes later we were all sitting down to a bounty of fried chicken, mashed potatoes and gravy, and all the trimmings, including home made bread and pie. It was the first real meal we had had for nearly a week and we never appreciated one more, before or since.

By the middle of the afternoon everything was arranged so we could live comfortably in our temporary home. The ladies had gone home, and Mamma, Mrs. Delaney, and the younger siblings decided to take a nap. Since the weather had improved somewhat, my sister, Elizabeth, and I, went on a sight-seeing hike with some of our newfound friends. The Hamre kids took us down to a small reservoir that had been created by the railroad embankment. Although the water was low at that time of the year, there was still enough to attract a small flock of wild ducks that seemed to show no fear of us as they swam at the far end of the pond.

Our next quest was our new home, located about fifty yards east of the main street and directly across from the Hamre residence. The carpenters, Joe Rasque and his father, Matt, were putting in their best licks to get the house to the stage where we could move in when our railroad car arrived. Although not as large as the home we had left in Palestine, the structure seemed quite roomy in comparison with the tarpaper-covered homestead shacks we had seen that morning coming through eastern Montana.

When we returned to the schoolhouse Mom had been to the store just across the road and bought a couple sacks of groceries to tide us over the few days until we could move into our new home. Someone had provided a two-burner coal oil stove and supper was almost ready as we walked in the door with our youthful appetites hanging out. Dad had not yet returned and all of us were a bit apprehensive about what he may have found at the Adams home. We hadn't long to wonder when, shortly after we finished eating, Hubert Morris rode up to the school yard gate, tied his horse to the fence, and walked rapidly up to the door. For the second time that day he came to us with unhappy tidings.

"The Doctor won't be home tonight," were his first words as he proceeded to tell us Dad had found a very sick man when he arrived at the ranch. The Reverend was in a coma. Although he had roused long enough to recognize Dad, it was only a temporary condition. He had again lost consciousness before Hubert left the ranch. When administration of available remedies seemed ineffective Dad and the family had decided to call in Dr. Garberson from Miles City.

A telegram from the railroad station at Sumatra resulted in the doctor's decision to make the 100 mile trip on Milwaukee train, No. 15, the following morning.

A little weary from the long trip and the ordeals of the day, the Midgett family retired early that Friday night hoping for better things in the morning. It was not to be the case for, a few minutes after seven A.M. we were awakened by a knock on the door followed immediately by Hubert's third appearance within twenty-four hours.

"Charles passed away a little after three this morning. He never regained consciousness." Hubert's voice was full of emotion. "The Doctor is getting a little sleep after being with him right up to the last. He will be coming down here sometime this afternoon after discussing plans for the funeral."

He continued in a subdued tone to tell us a wire had been sent to Dr. Garberson with the latest information so he would not make an unnecessary trip. Of course it was very sad news to all of us, since, for the past year or more, we had looked anxiously toward our association with the good pastor and his family.

With all the bad news of the past twenty-four hours—first the sad and untimely death of our friend and benefactor, then the unfavorable information concerning our new home and the immigrant car, and now Dad's enforced absence from his family—our second day in Montana was not a particularly happy one. Although my mother tried to hide her true feelings from us kids, I detected an air of sadness and disillusionment. In fact, if she ever showed any sign of homesickness in Montana it was during those first few days in Hibbard. Within a week the ordinary demands of her family were sufficient to overcome such feelings and from then on she was prepared to face whatever our new life held in store.

Undoubtedly, the greatest single factor in alleviating the situation was Dad's return to the household. We were very glad to see him when he arrived about two o'clock that Saturday afternoon. Although still tired from the train ride and the night's ordeal, he spent the rest of the afternoon at the new house helping the carpenters who labored from sunrise to sunset, six days a week. They were just as eager to complete the job as we were and some of the neighbors turned out to help during those last few days.

Arrangements were made with a mortuary in Forsyth to take care of Reverend Adams' body. The funeral services were scheduled for Tuesday morning with burial on a small hillock in the northwest quarter of the home section, about 200 yards from the ranch house.

All of us except the two younger children, Robert and Olive, rode to the funeral with Joe Rasque. The graveside service was attended by a large gathering of neighbors from as far as fifteen miles around even though there were no means of communication except that of person to person, and transportation was by horsedrawn vehicles. The sermon was delivered by Reverend Fred C. Fulford, the Methodist Minister at Forsyth.

This was the first opportunity for Mother to meet Mrs. Adams (Sallie) who insisted we stay for dinner that had been brought in by some of the close neighbors, the Charley Burnetts, who lived on the east half of the same section, and the Ross Dorothys and Ernest Stevens, who adjoined them on the south and southwest. Apparently most of those present at the funeral had heard of our arrival and, although it was a somber occasion, Dad and Mom were happy to meet many of their future friends and neighbors, several of whom were to become Dad's patients during the next ten years.

Chapter III

Wednesday, the 17th of October, 1914, was a red letter day. In the afternoon, the local freight train running between Miles City and Harlowton set off on the railroad siding a car bearing the initials I.C.R.R., which we knew had to be ours. Before we could get there Billy Cook had opened the car door from the inside and jumped to the ground to greet Elizabeth and me. After almost two weeks the rest of our entourage—Daisy, the cow, and Cricket, our little bay mare—had arrived along with all our other worldly possessions. Our happiness was even more complete when Dad announced that Mr. Rasque told him we could start moving into our new house the next morning even though there was still quite a lot of work to be done.

By evening of the following day, with the help of four or five of our wonderful neighbors and their horses and wagons, everything was moved, and we were quite comfortably settled. A rough two-stall shed had been hastily thrown up for the livestock after we arrived and, of course, the usual two-holer out behind the house was ready for occupancy. Daisy and Cricket were at least temporarily protected from the elements of the late Montana fall.

Little did we realize then that this would be our home for less than a year. Dad had planned to live in Hibbard and either drive back and forth the two and one-half miles to carry on what farming operations he may have had in mind or hire someone to put in the crops in the spring and harvest them in the fall. How his plans were changed so quickly after our arrival has always been somewhat of a mystery to me, but I never talked to him about it.

Probably the one object Dad was most glad to see unloaded from the railroad car was his 1912 Model T. During those first few days he had been called on to render his medical services at least a half dozen times and in all except one case he made the trips in rigs provided by people who came after him. With distances ranging from five to twenty miles, most of the day was spent in travel from the time he left home until he returned.

That he was not yet licensed to practice medicine in Montana never seemed to enter Dad's mind. At least he did not let it deter him from answering calls for his services. He had applied for his license before leaving Illinois and, since the two states were on a reciprocity basis, he assumed he would soon receive his certificate from the state medical department. However, up to that time he had heard nothing about it.

After another week of getting settled, we all began to feel at home in Montana. School resumed as soon as we had moved out of the schoolhouse, and Betty and I became pupils of the fifth and seventh grades with Mrs. Adams as our teacher. The one-room, eight-grade school was a new experience for us but we soon adjusted and became acquainted with the other kids.

A Sunday School had been organized a year earlier by the Reverend Adams and other settlers in the area. My folks, strongly religious, soon became quite active in the services. Following the death of her husband, Mrs. Adams attempted to carry on church services with the help of other interested and dedicated people of the community. Dad was soon active as superintendent of the Sunday School and even preached a sermon or two when the minister was unable to come to Hibbard.

Once a month, weather favorable, Reverend Fulford came up from Forsyth to Sumatra by train on Sunday morning to preach at the eleven o'clock service. He made the five-mile trip on over to Hibbard by horse and buggy driven by one of the Adams and held services at three o'clock in the afternoon following a basket dinner in which all of those who came to Sunday School or church partook.

Since No. 16, the train going east in the evening, did not stop at Hibbard, the Reverend usually stayed over Sunday night with a congregation family and returned to Forsyth the next morning on No. 18, the Columbian. We were usually the host family because we lived near the station and had more room than most households. We were happy to have him, came to know him very well, and developed a high regard for him during the next two years. As the weather became cold in our area church services were discontinued until spring.

It didn't take long for us to settle into a more or less regular routine. Within two weeks after moving into our house the interior work was completed. Mother was happy to move her furniture from the bedroom in which it had been stacked, lay her carpets, and begin to live again instead of merely camping first in one room and then another as they were finished. The two stoves, one in the kitchen and the other in the living room, the dining table, and a couple of beds were about the only permanent articles of furniture until after the first of November. We kids had been sleeping on the floor near the big heater and were glad to move to our nice warm soft feather beds again.

The construction wasn't completed any too soon when, on the ninth of November, we had our first opportunity to see what a Montana cold wave and snow storm was like. Since it was the first of the season and also the first the Midgett family had experienced, it made a strong and lasting impression on me. Perhaps it was the suddenness of the storm's onslaught that produced the greatest effect at the time. We had never seen anything like it in southern Illinois. There winter was comparatively mild and most of the snow turned into a cold rain before it subsided.

It was a Wednesday, the middle of our third week in school following Mr. Adams' death. The late fall weather had been as beautiful as autumn in Montana can be. It was crisp and cool at night but warmed up to a temperature of 55 or 60 degrees by the middle of the afternoon. Day after day of beautiful sunshine and limitless blue skies stretched as far as the eye could see. Truly this part of Montana was "Big Sky Country," as the state came to be called years later. If anyone had told us that Wednesday morning our beautiful weather was coming to an end we would have been very reluctant to believe them. It was a morning just like a dozen others preceding it.

In 1914 forecasting and early warning of changes in weather did not exist in that part of Montana. Modern methods of communication that make it possible to know the state of the weather five miles or five thousand miles away were still in very early stages of development. It would be another ten or fifteen years before the simplest radio set was made available to the average family. Even that made little difference to people of this area since they were too far away to receive signals from the few weak transmitters in Billings and Miles City.

Thus, no advance warning or report of any kind prepared us for what was already on its way when Elizabeth and I went tramping off to school that beautiful fall morning, confident it was going to be another day like those we had enjoyed during our first weeks in Montana. By noon, when we went home to lunch, it was still around 50 above zero and, although the sun was shining brightly a bank of gray clouds was visible low in the western sky a hundred miles away. Mrs. Adams had noticed the change in weather during the noon hour and announced that we should keep a sharp lookout on that approaching cloud formation. By two o'clock, a light northwest wind came up, the sun disappeared, and the clouds began to spit light flakes of snow. Since we all wore light clothing, Mrs. Adams was quite concerned about our welfare and kept a close eye on the thermometer outside one of the south windows. By three o'clock the temperature dropped to 30 and the snow was becoming thicker, whipped by an increasingly strong wind out of the northwest. Since the days were quite short and it had begun to turn dark early, Mrs. Adams decided to dismiss school and let us kids go home before the storm got much worse. During the next two hours the wind increased greatly, the thermometer dropped to 20, and the snow thickened to the point where visibility was cut to a few yards. We were experiencing our first Montana blizzard and it was anything but a pleasant event.

It was still quite early for winter weather and by morning the storm had passed with no serious consequences. Only three or four inches of snow had fallen. Although the wind had blown foot-and-a-half drifts in the coulees, the dirt roads remained clear and those kids who had to walk home were met by their parents. Most of the settlers had seen these storms before and recognized the signs of this one in plenty of time to round up the small number of cattle and horses in the area.

We were glad it wasn't any worse. There was still much work to do around the house before we were ready for winter. Dad had made arrangements with D.W. Peyton and his brother, Oscar, with the help of Billy Cook, to furnish us with a couple cords of split wood. He also purchased two or three tons of Roundup coal from the Rasques, who hauled it from the railroad car and dumped it into the bin in our cellar. Hay and grain for Daisy and Cricket were procured from the elevator at Sumatra and Hubert Morris and his nephew, Morris Adams, hauled them by wagon to the small storage shed that we had finished just before the storm hit.

Our food problem had been pretty well provided for before leaving Illinois. Barrels and boxes had been filled with canned fruits and vegetables, smoked and dried meats and other prepared foods. Dad had learned while on his trip to Montana that prices of practically everything were much higher than those in Illinois. Mother was very busy the last two or three months before leaving, canning and preserving fresh fruit and vegetables, most from our two-acre orchard and garden. This was greatly supplemented by contributions from relatives and friends who had loaded two barrels of food in the immigrant car at the last minute as a surprise going-away present. So, we were well assured of something to eat for at least our first year in Montana.

One of the most serious problems we encountered from the beginning was finding a water supply, both for the family and the livestock. We learned this was not peculiar to us, nor did the situation improve greatly during the ten years the folks lived in the area. Upon inquiry, we learned water for drinking was available from two sources—a shallow well dug in the school yard and a cistern near the station house which was filled from a wooden tank car brought in about once a week on the local freight train as a service of the rail company.

There wasn't much choice between the two; both had a very strong and unsavory taste—alkali from the well and decaying wood from the car. However, we soon became used to it and, since it did us no apparent harm, we drank it. Water for Daisy and Cricket was provided by the little pond made by the railroad embankment, but in winter holes had to be cut through the ice to get to it. When snow became plentiful from the middle of December on, we kids spent many hours filling the reservoir of the kitchen range and a boiler on top of the stove. This was the purest water we had and it was a treat to drink water free of pungent flavors.

Snow from the first storm was mostly gone by Thanksgiving and the 1914-15 winter of remained relatively mild. Mrs. Delaney and Billy Cook stayed with us all winter which helped a great deal in keeping us from missing our friends and relatives back east.

   *   *   *   *

Although the word "priority" was hardly ever heard in those days Dad was faced with many different tasks before the freeze-up in December. His first choice was to provide a supply of stock water up on the ranch. A few days after Billy Cook arrived he and Dad began the construction of an earthen dam across a shallow draw running south through the east edge of section 17 about a quarter of a mile below the site of the house that would be built a year later. Since we did not yet have any work horses, Dad borrowed a pair of good 1600 pounders from Mrs. Adams. For the next ten days Billy was busy scooping out a basin about 100 yards long, 100 feet wide, and eight feet deep at the dam's face with an overflow culvert through its east end. Modern machinery would easily complete the job in less than two days, but when man and horse power were the only kinds available, time was a most important factor.

This masterpiece of engineering skill, dug out and piled up a scoopful at a time, turned out to be one of the most important creations of Dad's and Billy's efforts. Since it was right on the south section line the dam became a part of the main road between Hibbard and Sumatra. All the east and west traffic between Roundup and Forsyth ran directly across the top of it during the next two or three years until a gravel road was built by the state north of the railroad right-of-way. Its most important function, however, was to hold back water from the runoff of melting snow in the spring and the very infrequent rains that fell during the spring, summer, and fall, thus providing stock water most of the year.

The other high priority job taking most of Dad's and Billy's time before winter set in was fencing the south half of Section 17. The north half was quite rough and broken by coulees, where a few potholes provided water for roving livestock until about the first of July. This area was never fenced except by the barbed wire separating the north and south halves of the section.

The Adams and the Burnetts, who had homesteaded the west and east halves of Section 20 just south of our land, had enclosed their places two years earlier, so their north line fence was also our south boundary. This left a half mile of fence on the north side that had to be built during the fall and the following spring so the 1915 crops could be protected from ranging stock.

Fences in those days were also built with nothing but manpower and horse-power from start to finish and it took many times the hours the same job would require today. The whole job required approximately 280 posts, set about two rods apart. The holes were all dug by hand to a depth of 15 to 18 inches. In easy digging five or six holes an hour was the limit. In rocky soil two to three holes was the product of sixty minutes of hard labor. They probably averaged little more than 30 to 35 posts set per day with one man digging the holes and the other setting and tamping the posts. By December first the ground had frozen too hard to continue but over 200 posts were in place. Stringing wire would have to wait until early spring.

* * * *

Despite four months of short days and long nights, time never seemed to drag for the Midgetts. With four children, two of them pre-schoolers, and two extra people in the household, Mother was busy from early morning until late at night just preparing meals, washing dishes, changing beds, and keeping all of us in clean clothes. Her load was lightened considerably by Mrs. Delaney, particularly by her attention to and care of the two little ones during the day. Other chores were shared among the family, with each member doing those things best suited to his or her size and ability. Mother was always a fastidious person—her house reflected this—and those around her were expected to reflect her concern.

In addition to my usual assignment of homework (Teacher Adams always gave us plenty), my time after school was taken up with a number of chores. It was my job to keep the stove reservoir and the water bucket filled, so I made at least three trips a day to the railroad cistern about 150 yards away. During weekends, extra trips were necessary to fill the wash tubs and boiler in preparation for wash day, which always fell on Monday. In the house, since heating for cooking and warmth was provided by wood and coal stoves, another job of mine was to keep the wood box and coal scuttle filled. With Dad working late at the ranch or away on sick calls, the evening task of milking Daisy often fell to me. A young Collie pup named Teddy, given to us by the Adams a few days after we arrived in Montana, was soon trained to help bring in the cow, saving one or more of us a half hour's ride on Cricket every evening. Elizabeth, although only ten years old, made herself very helpful to her mother by taking care of the two little ones after school hours. She also regularly helped with the dishes.

On weekends, Elizabeth and I often rode double on Cricket, visiting one or more of the families whose children attended the Hibbard school. One of these families, the D. W. Paytons, who lived about two miles south of the village, had five children who walked in to school every day. They were Howard, Hazel, and Helen Payton and Frances and Lola Davis, the latter two, daughters of D.W.'s second wife. Other children attending the Hibbard school that year were the two Rasque boys, Moody and Johnny, Florence and Laura Jackson, Morris and Opal Adams, Arthur Hamre, Gladys Payton and her little brother. I recall two of the Stockland girls were there, too, making a total of about twenty pupils in the eight grades taught by Mrs. Adams.

One episode stemming from these visits is still fresh in my mind. It wasn't long before I began to notice Hazel was a little different from the other girls in school and she was worth some special attention. A year younger than I, she had a very pretty face with big blue eyes and was "pleasingly plump." It wasn't long before I began to carry her books up around Rattlesnake Butte on our way home after school. This led to the frequent visits by Elizabeth and I to their place on the weekends.

One Saturday morning after Thanksgiving, I asked Mamma if I could go out to the Paytons. Satisfied that my chores had been taken care of she readily gave her consent on condition that I come home before dark—about five o' clock at that season of the year. Billy Cook had driven Cricket up to the ranch that morning, so my only way to get there was by "shank's mares"—on foot, over the ridges (this was a common expression in those days—and also a common mode of travel). There was only a light skiff of snow left on the ground and a bright warm sun in the sky and I was able to make good time, covering the two and one-half miles in little more than a half hour, arriving just as they were sitting down to dinner. Mrs. Payton apologized that they were just finishing the remains of Thanksgiving dinner, but as is usually true of farm families, the table was heaped with a variety of goodies that I greatly enjoyed.

Most of the afternoon was spent playing outdoor games such as hide and seek, dare base, pum-pum-pullaway and others. An hour or more of horseback riding took up most of the rest of the afternoon and it was time for me to start for home. If only I had—but for some reason I didn't. As we walked from the barn to the house I was attracted to the woodpile where a tool that I thought to be an ax was stuck in a big log. With a typical twelve year old boy's yen to impress the girls and especially <u>this</u> girl, I jumped up on the log to pull out the imbedded tool. I was surprised when, instead of an ax, it turned out to be a wood adze, the first one I had ever seen. The girls walked on into the house while I decided to try my hand with the new toy. On the first chop the blade slipped through a knot in the log and ended up in my overshoe, shoe (we wore high ones in those days), sock and the inside of my left ankle bone.

Without waiting to say good-bye to my hosts or even taking time to examine myself to determine the extent of my injury, I took off for home where I knew I could get the best medical attention. Although the ankle seemed to be numb, I could feel the blood squishing in my shoe as I trudged along the ruts where I had stepped lightly in the opposite direction that morning. The sun had set in all its colorful glory, but I was in no mood to appreciate it. I was more than glad to see the dim light from the coal oil laps as I rounded the big hill and limped down the two hundred yard grade to our house.

It was totally dark when I walked in the back door and relieved my mother's anxiety. By the time Dad came in with his lantern from milking the cow, she had removed my blood-soaked shoe and sock and cleaned my foot of the gory mess. Thanks to a doctor dad, I was soon bandaged up and on my way to a quick recovery without even a two dollar charge for a house call. I never played with a wood adze again, but sixty years later I still have the scar on my left ankle.

*   *   *   *

Recreation and entertainment in 1914 in this thinly populated and pristine country was pretty much the product of individual imagination and ingenuity. There were no theaters, no bowling alleys, no organized football, basketball, or baseball leagues, no radios or TVs to sit in front of four or five hours a day—in fact no form of ready-made pastime or recreation to occupy the few spare hours of an occasional weekend or infrequent stormy day. This was no great inconvenience during the growing season when farmers worked twelve to sixteen hours a day, but Montana winters, with their short days and long cold nights, left lots of time for contemplation and recreation.

Winter was upon us, and various recreation ideas were proposed at a public meeting called at the school house early in November. Among the suggestions for a community entertainment program was the organization of a band, dances, and amateur night programs, including spelldowns, ciphering matches, and other tests of mental ability in which anyone who wished could participate.

Band practice started early in December and was held on Sunday afternoons at the school house. It was a big surprise to all of us when more than fifteen horn blowers and string sawers showed up for the first practice. I remember a few of them were two of the Rasque brothers, Joe and Moody, and Joe and Jim Cosgrove, and a little later, twin brothers, Carl and Clay Buchan. Public dances, probably the most popular form of amusement in those days, were held once or twice a month in the little country schoolhouses on Saturday nights. Amateur nights, with a variety of acts, were held every second and fourth Friday nights of each month at the Hibbard school. Both Mother and Dad were quite talented; I remember two renditions by the latter at these programs. He had a very fine baritone voice, and I can still hear him sing "Asleep in the Deep" and dramatically reciting a short reading entitled "The Potato Bug". Another of his favorite musical selections was "Silver Threads Among the Gold" which they sang as a duet.

Since my parents were such devout Methodists, Saturday night dances were off limits to us kids. We spent most weekend nights at home, where entertainment was pretty much a family affair. Most of our evenings, after chores and school homework, were spent playing such exciting games as Flinch, Bunco, Parcheesi, and Old Maid. The carom board, on which a number of games can be played, was also very popular. Dad was usually the winner, but he let the rest of us win once in a while. The intricacies of checkers were also heated contests a couple of evenings each week, but chess was a little complicated for kids our ages. Since we all had fairly good voices and enjoyed singing, we spent many hours gathered around the piano we had brought with us to Montana. Elizabeth and I had taken music lessons for two years before moving, and we still practiced once in a while. Regular playing cards, with their games of Pinochle, Poker, Rummy, etc., were instruments of the Devil and, to my knowledge, there was never a deck of regular playing cards in my parents' home.

Outdoor activities during the winter were limited for a number of reasons. Below freezing weather and heavy snow made hiking and horseback riding almost impossible. Without mountains and large bodies of water we could not do much skiing and ice skating. We did have lots of fun sliding down the low hills south and east of Hibbard, and the little pond made by the railroad embankment provided some skating after we had scraped off the layer of snow.

Dad bought me a .22 rifle shortly after we arrived in Montana and we spent many weekends hunting cottontails and jackrabbits, which were very plentiful. The latter turned out to be an important item in our diet, providing a large part of fresh meat during our first winter. We had been warned regarding the incidence of tularemia among rabbits, but if they were dressed out while still warm the danger was greatly reduced. Sage hens were also abundant and were comparable in size to full-grown chickens. Mother usually ground the wild meat and made sandwiches for the Sunday afternoon dinners before church services. Their tastiness was attested to by the fact that there were never any left to take home.

Mother had little time for recreation and diversions, seldom participating in the pastimes the rest of us enjoyed so much. She was a good seamstress and kept her foot-treadle sewing machine busy most of the time, making and mending clothes for herself, Dad and us four children. Since boys in those days wore knee breeches until they were fifteen or sixteen years old, we all wore full-length stockings, usually made of cotton. They wore out quickly, and Mom spent many hours with her darning ball and needle putting patches on patches to prolong their wear. Her only diversion from the regular routine of washing dishes, cooking meals, and all the other daily tasks, came during the weekend, when she attended and often took part in the Friday night get-togethers. On weekends, none of us ever missed Sunday services. Such a regimen would seem to many people to be a big "grind" but for her, consecration to her religion and dedication of service to her family mitigated most of the drudgery of her days of menial and tiring labor.

Chapter IV

Time passed quickly and uneventfully during November and December of the first year. The Christmas season was, of course, the highlight. The traditional Christmas program was presented by the pupils as a part of a community celebration on Friday night before Christmas. A fir tree was decorated with strings of popcorn and cranberries, chains of colored paper rings, and dozens of multicolored candles. A red clad Santa Claus with a long, white beard was there in the person of my dad and treats were given to all the kids. The newly organized band rendered its first concert of four or five numbers and everybody had a good time.

Our family Christmas, although a little short on gifts, was also enjoyable. With no general stores within fifty miles, the folks ordered all their Christmas gifts from Sears, Roebuck and Co. in Chicago. Somehow the large package arrived and was hidden away with none of us kids seeing it. Our folks always put up a trimmed tree a week or so before the holidays but no gifts were ever put under it until Christmas Eve after we were all in bed and sound asleep.

Of course Elizabeth and I knew what to expect but the two younger siblings still met Christmas morning with great amazement. It was quite a thrill to see Robert's and Olive's eyes bug out when they peeked into the living room and frantically tried to open their gifts. Other than a couple of small toys for each of us, most of our presents consisted of articles of winter clothing—pants, dresses, sweaters, caps, mittens, and heavy underwear.

Turkeys were scarce in eastern Montana in those days and most people dined on home-cured ham or pork roasts for their Christmas feast. At our house these were accompanied by the customary mashed potatoes, dressing and gravy, plus three or four vegetables such as squash, yams, corn or string beans. This bountiful repast was topped off by a big piece of mince or pumpkin pie with a large dipper of home made ice cream on top.

Every meal at our house was preceded by Dad saying "grace," but on this special day his thirty-second ritual was extended to more than a minute by his offer of thanks to the Almighty for good health, good friends, and the good weather we had enjoyed up to this time. With dinner over and the tummies full of good food, Dad and Billy soon found their favorite rockers and, within minutes, were sawing it off. Mom and Mrs. Delaney stacked the dishes in the sink and, after putting the two little ones down for their naps, took the short stroll over to the Hamres, our nearest neighbors. Elizabeth and I spent the rest of the afternoon skating on the little pond with eight or ten other kids in the neighborhood.

All in all, our first three months in Montana were very enjoyable. The weather had been favorable for much of the work on the ranch; the dam was completed and more of the fencing finished than had been expected. Dad hadn't been rushed in his medical practice, but he had officiated at the arrival of a couple of new eight pound citizens that, of course, took place in their mothers' bedrooms. With a hospital fifty miles away and transportation always a serious problem, these little fellers were truly home products. Despite the lack of most of the sanitary precautions prevalent today, a very high percentage of Dad's products survived their infancy and grew into normal, healthy kids and teenagers.

The New Year of 1915 opened with considerably colder weather. January and February brought heavy snows with strong northwest winds that piled up six to eight foot drifts in unprotected areas. There were no state or county programs for clearing the very inadequate dirt roads after a heavy storm, and the modes of transportation underwent a radical change in winter. When necessary, most travel was either by horseback or sled. I vividly remember Dad attired in about twenty-five pounds of warm clothing: a full-length sheepskin coat, fur cap with ear flaps, wool muffler, heavy gloves, long wool sox, and his high six-buckle overshoes. Then he trudged out to the shed where he saddled Cricket, hooked his pill bags over the pommel, and started out to one of the many five to ten mile trips he was to make during the next several years. Warm weather trips on muddy roads were made by the same little mare hitched to the single-seat, two-wheel cart that we had brought along in our immigrant car.

The first real chinook that spring struck our area early in March and the high banks of ice and snow began to thaw. By April the sun had grown warmer and the little gullies began to run with rivulets from melted snow, gradually filling the new reservoir that would provide stock water for the next twelve months.

With the coming of spring, two or three big jobs demanded Dad's immediate attention. His first choice was the completion of a half mile of the fence on the east side. He and Billy resumed where they had left off as soon as the frost was out of the ground. It was still early to start the spring plowing for the melting snow and early April rains had thoroughly soaked the ground and left the heavy gumbo soil too sticky to turn over.

The problem of finding a pair of large work horses turned out to be much more difficult than Dad had expected. During the winter he had contacted most of our close neighbors. Since most of them had been in the west only two or three years themselves, few surplus farm animals, either horses or cattle, had yet been produced. Mrs. Adams suggested the Herbolds, who had one of the older and larger spreads out south of Sumatra, might have a team or two they would sell. So one Saturday in late March he and I drove the ten miles to their ranch hoping Dad could ride one horse and lead the other back to the Adams place while I returned by car. Again, we were disappointed when the ranch foreman refused to part with any animals.

It wasn't until early April that the much needed horses were procured. Dad and Billy took the train to Miles City, then known as the "horse capital of the world." Monthly sales held at Fort Keogh were the largest in existence and Dad was lucky enough to bid on a nice pair of bay 1600-pounders with harness for $275. "Bob" and "Barney" made the hundred-mile trip in a freight car to Sumatra, where they were hitched to a new Studebaker farm wagon that Dad had bought from Tom Brown's implement company. At the same time he purchased a two-share mole-board plow and disk and pulled them out to the ranch behind the wagon.

During the next two weeks about fifty acres of nice sod in the southwest quarter of Section 17 were turned over for the first time. After disking and harrowing, the newly cultivated land was sown to Durum spring wheat and by May 10 the dark green shoots of Dad's first crop in Montana began to pop through the moist soil. By the middle of May another 25 or 30 acres were broken and planted to corn and oats for feed. With much sunny weather during the next three weeks, all the newly planted crops got off to a good start.

Adequate rainfall in late June and early July assured the crop. Except for cultivation of the corn to clean out Russian thistles, which had become a regional pest over the past four or five years, most of the farm work was finished until harvest time. Since this was virgin soil, insect pests were not a serious menace and the only remaining threat to a bountiful crop, a destructive hail storm, did not develop during the rest of the growing season.

Although the winter had not seemed long, we were all glad when the spring days lengthened and the sun climbed higher in the sky, giving off more life-giving heat and energy to wake and stimulate the action and growth of living things. By the middle of April, the natural grasses were turning from the brown of winter to a light, rich green, and the sagebrush that covered thousands of acres was changing its light gray to the bluish-green which it would wear all summer.

The abundant animal life, including field mice, prairie dogs, and cottontails, was emerging from the winter to look for sources of food for themselves and the baby crop that always showed up this time of year. Rattlesnakes came out of their rock caverns on the surrounding hills and sought the warmth of the lower areas. Rattler-hunting posses organized in the community and killed nearly fifty of the reptiles ranging from little wrigglers to four-footers with seven to ten rattles.

Prairie dogs numbered in the thousands in eastern Montana, and western Rosebud County had more than its fair share. They lived in colonies, more commonly known as towns, that sometimes covered four or five square miles. In many areas they were thick enough to destroy large tracts of small grain. One colony occupied a large part of Section 1, just east of the Hibbard town site, and extended over into adjacent sections, one of which was owned by the Jackson family. The Jacksons were in-laws of the Rasques. Both had emigrated west from Minnesota in 1912 and had homesteaded diagonally across the railroad section on which the village was located. Even though his 1914 wheat crop had been a good one, Mr. Jackson estimated he had lost a hundred or more bushels to the prairie dogs. Despite his spreading large quantities of poisoned grain around the colony in the fall, the spring crop of the little animals seemed to be as large as ever, as they made their appearance with the warm weather.

With my new .22 rifle my favorite hunting quarry became the prairie dog. Mr. Jackson made me a proposition to furnish ammunition and pay me five cents for every tail of the little pests I could bring him. However, I didn't make much money, and within a couple of weeks he withdrew his offer. Although I think I killed quite a few of the varmints, it was nearly impossible to catch them out in the open. When anyone was within sight they sat scolding on the mounds next to their burrows; even when hit by a bullet, they would make it into their holes. That rather brief experience completely discouraged me from ever becoming a big (or little) game hunter.

* * * *

Two sad events occurring that spring affected the lives of at least three families in the community. The first of these was when our Collie pup, Teddy, grown into a fine cattle dog, was hit by train No. 15, while trying to drive some cows off the track after they wandered onto the right-of-way. It was a Saturday morning and I had just started over to help him, but I was a minute too late. He died a few minutes after I got to him, but his body was not mangled. The whole family took it rather hard, especially the two little ones, who had grown very fond of the dog as he had of them.

Since he was a beautiful and intelligent dog, we had his hide mounted. For years it hung in the house at the ranch. Of course, we had to have another dog. As luck would have it Teddy's mother was due for another litter in just a few weeks. Mrs. Adams gave us our pick of the brood and Teddy II soon grew up to be as beautiful and intelligent as his predecessor. Next to old Cricket, he became the favorite animal of our domestic menagerie.

The second event was truly a tragedy for our friends and neighbors, the Jacksons and the Rasques. One weekday morning in May they were greatly shocked to receive a telegram from Pipestone, Minnesota, stating that the eldest daughter of the Jacksons, Pearl, was attacked, bound by her assailant, and burned to death in a fire that destroyed the Northern Pacific depot, where she was the night operator. The remains of her body had been found after the fire cooled down enough to allow a search of the ruins.

Mr. and Mrs. Jackson and Mrs. Rasque left on the next train for Pipestone. After burial of the girl's remains, they stayed for a week to aid the law officers in their attempt to determine motives and locate her slayer. They returned to Montana without any definite clues to his identity. To my knowledge the culprit was never caught, but we learned how events occurring many miles away can come to touch our own lives.

That fall after the harvest, the Jackson family sold their place and returned to Minnesota to help clear up the case. Although no clear solution ever developed, the official assumption was that a transient had left a passing freight and probably attacked the girl when she refused to let him stay in the depot. He then set fire to the building to cover his crime. We were sorry to lose the Jacksons. They were intelligent, hard-working folks. Although not experienced farmers, they had already established a very successful operation in the three years they had been in the area.

A third event that affected us, especially Olive, was the decision of Mrs. Delaney to go back home about the first of June. Olive was three years old and had grown accustomed to having Mrs. Delaney's every attention from the time she was born. It was inevitable that the sudden departure would leave a big void in her young life. The rest of us tried to make it up to her by giving her more of our love and attention. Mother's burden became somewhat heavier than usual, but Elizabeth took up the slack by assuming the care of her little sister when not in school.

*   *   *   *

The big community event that summer, the 4th of July celebration, was staged at Bascom, a little village about five miles west of Hibbard. This was one of the few holidays of the year in this frontier land and all usual activities were abandoned for the day. Settlers from near and far traveled by every type of conveyance available, horse and buggy, team and wagon, horseback, and the few Model Ts that had made their appearance in our area. Even a few bicycles were in evidence, although they were still a rather scarce article.

The few business houses in Bascom were decorated with flags and bunting, and the day's program consisted of foot races, horse races, and a bucking horse contest among the amateur cowboys living in the area. Although forty years old, Dad showed his prowess as an athlete by winning the 100 yard dash in the thirty-five years and older group. I took second in the upper grade boy's race, and Elizabeth got a white ribbon for a third place in the younger girls' 50 yard dash.

Most of the two or three hundred families who attended the big affair brought their own lunches. We all ate together at long tables constructed by laying twelve-inch planks on four-foot saw horses. To slake the thirst, tubs of lemonade and iced tea were provided, and fifty or sixty gallons of ice cream were doled out in scoopfuls for dessert. As usual, a few blithe spirits in the happy crowd provided their own refreshments or frequently patronized the saloon. Late in the afternoon, the big gathering heard the announcement that a wire had been received that Jess Willard, the latest "white hope," had defeated Jack Johnson for the heavyweight boxing championship of the world.

There was little restriction of fireworks, and their use by the kids was controlled only by parents. All day long, the popping of small firecrackers could be heard around town. After dark, the climax of the big celebration was an exhibition of sky rockets, Roman candles, sparklers, and pin wheels, occasionally accentuated by the explosion of a giant cracker. The big day ended with a free dance in the Bascom school house, attended by more than a hundred "trippers of the light fantastic," most of whom stayed until daylight. There must have been many tired feet and aching heads the next morning, but the Fourth of July only comes once a year and there weren't too many ways for these simple folk to enjoy themselves.

*   *   *   *

Two interesting adventures occurred at Hibbard in summer and fall—at least interesting personally because nothing like them had ever happened to me before. With ample spring rainfall the grass cover during the summer grew very heavy and, by the middle of August, had matured and was very dry. One Sunday afternoon the church service was interrupted by a cry of "fire." Rushing out, we could smell the smoke blowing in from the west. Further investigation of the source of the smoke showed a prairie fire about a mile west and traveling rapidly southeastward along a coulee on a two hundred yard front. We all grabbed shovels, hoses, and wet sacks and ran for the fire. By the time we got there, about fifteen or twenty men had already gathered. Within an hour the blaze had been stopped, just before it reached the scrubby pine growth southwest of town. Investigation later showed the fire had started from sparks thrown out by a passing locomotive. It was an exciting afternoon, but we had a glimpse of the danger to small towns like ours from prairie wildfires.

Later, in the fall, after the first flight of ducks had come to the area, I took my .22 and went to the railroad embankment at the north end of the reservoir to try to sneak up on a bird. After waiting fifteen or twenty minutes, a green teal swam up toward me about ten or fifteen yards away. Raising my rifle I aimed carefully and hit it on the first shot and the wind blew it into shore right at my feet.

As I reached to pick the duck out of the water I got the shock of my life when I saw a big rattlesnake only ten feet away swimming toward the dead bird. I recovered from my surprise quickly, and as it reached the bank I pointed the gun at a spot directly behind its head and pulled the trigger. Bullseye. The snake stopped suddenly, turned over on its back, and writhed vigorously.

The common belief was that snakes didn't die until the sun goes down, but it didn't take long for this one to quit wriggling. I reached down, pulled it out of the water, and looked it over. It was about four feet long and had ten rattles and a button, probably the largest rattler I have ever seen. The next day I skinned it, salted the inner surface, and hung it on the shed to dry. I intended to make a belt of it but something went wrong with my curing job, the skin smelled, and the belt never got done.

*   *   *   *

I believe the previous winter had been a time of serious contemplation and decision-making for Dad and Mother. Up to now, Dad's biggest dilemma had been the choice between continuing his career as a pill peddler in a sparsely populated land or assumption of the time-honored role as a tiller of the soil. His boyhood life on the farm had left an indelible imprint on him and now it was time to make a choice.

Despite the fine friendships and the enjoyable times we had, the little village of Hibbard did not seem to satisfy our needs. By spring Dad was beginning to talk of building a house up on his 640 acres. Although two or three new families had moved into the Hibbard community and three young men from Seattle, Harvey Hoffman and Carl and Clay Buchan, were building a new store on the north side of the railroad, there was no indication a town of any size would develop during the next few years. Probably the most important factors in Dad's final decision were three bumper harvests of wheat and oats in 1912, 1913, and 1914. By July 1915 he and Mother were drawing plans and plotting sites for the buildings to be erected on the ranch.

By mid-July, soil moisture and good growing weather had assured a good wheat crop. Dad and Billy spent most of their time at the ranch where there was plenty of work to be done. The fences had been completed, and a log framework had been set up for the new barn, later constructed on the brow of the hill facing east, toward both the dam and Sumatra, visible two miles away.

The plans for the ranch home were pretty well completed, and arrangements were made to start construction by August 1. Dad hired Rufus Jones and his brother Earl, who had been carpenters back in Iowa. They had come to Montana a year earlier to homestead in the Rattlesnake area, six or seven miles northwest of Hibbard. Lumber was purchased from the Midland Lumber Co. at Sumatra, managed by Henry Thayer, a tall, good-natured young fellow who had formerly worked for the same firm in Miles City.

Financial arrangements were made with the Sumatra Bank, a branch of the Wiley, Clark, and Greening system of banks in eastern Montana. Bob Ross, a very capable and personable young man, was also transferred from Miles City as cashier and manager. He developed a reputation as one of the better bankers in Montana and became one of Dad's best friends over the next few years.

Harvest time began about the middle of August, when the winter wheat crop had turned to a golden hue. Since Dad had planted spring wheat, our crop was cut and shocked nearly two weeks later. It was my first experience as a shocker, and I soon found following a binder drawn by four horses for ten hours a day was rather tiring for a thirteen year old, 110-pound boy. However, the inducement of a dollar a day was enough to keep Morris Adams and me on the job until it was done. By September 10 the big steam-powered Rumley tractor pulled up beside the barn framework with the even larger International Harvester threshing machine.

The barn was not yet finished. After putting on the roof and part of the rough siding, Dad decided to stretch a double layer of chicken wire around the post supports and have the straw from the thresher blown into it for warmth. A novel idea, it worked very well, and for the next two or three years each new crop of straw provided most of the protection for the stock housed in the barn. Each year the process was repeated, and our barn was probably one of the warmest in the area. Any excess straw was dropped on the roof, where it provided additional insulation from the cold of winter and the heat of summer.

Because our home on the ranch was not finished by threshing time, arrangements were made with Mrs. Adams and Mrs. Burnett to provided the noon meal for the threshing crew at the Adams place, only a half mile away. Of course, Mother was there to help prepare the meals and wash the dishes the two or three days while our crop was being threshed. Elizabeth stayed at home and took care of the two younger children. Most of the crew lived within two or three miles of our place, so they slept and ate breakfast and supper at home.

During those two days I worked as a spiker in the field as we stacked our grain. It was a hard job, but I enjoyed the challenge of tossing those heavy bundles up on the big racks that hauled them from the field to the thresher. Since there were no motor trucks yet, the threshed wheat was hauled to the elevator at Sumatra in double-sided wagons pulled by strong teams of horses. Because it was only about a four mile round trip, taking a little more than an hour and a half, only three or four teams and wagons were needed to take care of the job. With three drivers of the bundle wagons, three loaders, and at least four spikers, an engineer on the tractor, an operator of the threshing machine, a driver of the water tank, the whole crew totaled about fifteen, hard-working men, most of whom were farmers on the surrounding homesteads. It was the custom for farmers in the neighborhood to help each other, thereby solving the labor problem and eliminating considerable cost of harvesting the crops. Nobody paid their neighbors for the work they did even though some may have had larger crops than others. They figured it all averaged out in the long run. It was part of being a neighbor in this new country.

1915 was the second year of World War I and increased demand and diminished supply of food commodities was beginning to affect prices, especially of grain. Rapid price rises were a boon for us. Wheat, which sold for 75 to 80 cents a bushel in 1912, was now selling at the elevator for $1.50 to $2.00. Although he deplored the European struggle, Dad appreciated the increase in grain prices and the more than $2,500 that his 25 to 30 bushel per acre wheat crop brought in the fall. His expenses had been extraordinarily heavy during our first year in Montana, but this excellent return from the wheat crop enabled him to take care of a few of his debts and go into the winter in good shape.

The feed crops of oats and corn had also been good, so he was able to feed his horses and Daisy without buying feed for the winter. During the summer, he bought four, year-old, black and white belted Hampshire pigs. He built a pen and a wallow for them just below the hill on which the barn was located. The two barrows were fattened for slaughter as soon as the weather turned cold enough to keep the meat from spoiling. By the first of December, we were well supplied with fresh cured hams and bacons from our own smoke house, which had been built between the house and the barn.

By October 1 our new home had been boxed in and the interior finished enough to move into. A few days later, the inside sheeting and insulation were in place downstairs, and a stairway replaced the ladder from the living room up to the east bedroom on the second floor. The inside work upstairs was left for us to complete, but as long as we were there it was never finished. Whether succeeding occupants of the house ever completed it, I don't know. The downstairs was planned to contain two large rooms, the combination kitchen-dining room across the east end and a large living room with a door in the south wall. The partition between the rooms was never built, and the whole downstairs was just one big room with the chimney running up through the middle. Heat for the upstairs came from the chimney and up the stairway from the lower floor, so it wasn't always as warm up there as we might have liked.

After the crop was in and we had moved, the second of our original guests from Illinois, Billy Cook, who had done most of the work on the ranch, decided it was time to go back home. He had recently received a letter from his sister, Stella, who had worked for Mother a couple of weeks when Olive was born. He showed us the letter stating their mother was seriously ill and asking that Billy come home. We were sorry to lose him, for he had proved to be a dependable worker with considerable ingenuity and initiative. He was a good friend of the family and had also been a cheap employee, working more than a year for board and room, ten dollars a week, and all his work clothes. Billy would probably have stayed with us as long as we were on the ranch, had it not been for his mother's condition. When he left, Dad gave him a bonus of the cost of his railroad ticket home. We received a short letter from him a week or two later, but never heard from him again.

Chapter V

Although we had not intended it, our move to the ranch, just two and one-half miles away, nearly severed our relations with Hibbard and all the friends we had made during the year we had been in Montana. Dad was called for medical services from time to time but otherwise we seldom saw these people. Since the school term was only eight months long and didn't begin until October 1, Dad decided to put us in school in Sumatra, which had developed much faster than Hibbard.

Two other important factors in the move were Mrs. Adams' transfer to the teaching position at Sumatra and the rumor that a high school would probably be established there in another year or two. Leaving Hibbard meant the loss of quite a few of the young friends Betty and I had found both in and out of school. Of course I regretted not being able to see my girlfriend, Hazel, every school day as I had during the previous year. Since it was only three or four miles from our place to theirs I rode over there a few times during the fall months, but the young romance gradually faded.

Originally constructed in 1910 for use as the town hall, the school building in Sumatra was located at the north end of Main Street. It was a little larger than the one at Hibbard and contained just one room for all eight grades. However, the number of pupils nearly doubled that of Hibbard, and there were already clear indications of the need for a larger building and more classrooms.

Although movement of new settlers into the area adjacent to Sumatra had slowed by 1916, more businesses and more people to run them had increased the population of the little town. A weekly newspaper, the *Sumatra Record*, had been started in 1913 by Jack McCausland, later publisher of the Forsyth paper. In the spring of 1914, the *Record* was purchased by a young printer and his wife, Mr. and Mrs. Henry Polk, who came from Missouri.

In the fall two young fellows, Dick Imhoff and Ben Carlen, came from California and built a department store that was a credit to a small town like Sumatra. The Post Office was moved from the Mercantile to the front half of the north side of the new building and the two young merchants, both single, lived in three rooms attached to the rear to the structure. Four or five new homes were constructed in 1915 and 1916 and were occupied by families with from two to five children, most of school age.

We were soon very much at home on the ranch but there was still much work to be done before winter set in. The chicken house to the north of our new home had to be enclosed to fend off winter winds. It had been constructed so half was below ground level and windows on the south side allowed the winter sun to provide some natural warmth. Because the sun shines most of the daylight hours in that part of the country, warmth for the birds was not much problem. In extremely cold weather, a small kerosene heater was hung from the ceiling with a tin flue through the roof to exhaust the fumes.

To the east and below the chicken house a small, dirt-covered root cellar was constructed to store vegetables harvested from our small garden. Like the grain harvest, the garden produced a good crop. Dad and I had spent many long hours during the summer keeping the weeds down, watering the growing plants with a sprinkler can, and gathering the produce as it ripened. After Mom canned large quantities of corn, tomatoes and beans, most of the remaining vegetables, including potatoes, turnips, cabbage, carrots, and a few pumpkins, were stored in the new cellar. So, we had an adequate supply of vegetable foods all winter and well into the spring.

In this area most of the homestead land within ten to fifteen miles north and south of the Milwaukee railroad had been filed upon by 1915. Public land until 1909 when the Revised Homestead Act was passed, it was now divided into townships six miles square containing thirty-six sections of 640 acres each. All except two of the even numbered sections in each township were divided into 320 acre homesteads and offered to the public. The odd numbered sections in this area had been granted to the Northern Pacific railroad and receipts from their sale or lease were used to help pay the cost of its construction. Sections 16 and 36 were given to the state and were known as school sections. Any revenue derived from them was credited to the state public school fund and distributed to the schools.

Since most of the good homestead land in the area was gone by 1915, Dad bought railroad section 17 in Township 10 North, Range 33 east. Mrs. Adams and the Burnetts lived on adjoining Section 20 to the south and Mrs. Adams' brother and father had homesteaded the north half of Section 18 just west of us. Others who had settled in the same locality were the Dorothy brothers, Ross and Wright, the Schleders, the Weigels, and the Stevens, all to the south of us.

The south half of Section 8 to the north of us had been homesteaded in 1912 by a family named Wedeward who proved up on their claim in 1917 and left the state after their son, Karl, enlisted in the service. There was no one living between our place and Sumatra since Section 16 was a school section and Section 15 had been purchased by the Sumatra Townsite Co. The southeast quarter of the latter was subdivided for sale of lots for homes and business houses. In 1915 expectation was high that within ten years Sumatra would have a population of at least a thousand people.

*   *   *   *

A full year had now passed since we arrived in Montana and Dad still did not have his state license to practice medicine. His indecision about what he wanted to do—farm or doctor—made it less than an urgent issue. In spite of this, he continued to see all who called on him for medical attention. It was not until June 26, 1916, after passing a short oral examination by the state Board of Medical Examiners, that he received his license. But in 1915 most of Dad's time was devoted to the farm and raising grain had gradually taken over as his principal occupation. Billy Cook had broken fifty or sixty more acres of sod during the summer and most of it had been planted to winter wheat before he left for Illinois. After the 1915 crop was harvested the stubble was disked under to rot and mulch the soil during the winter for planting to feed grains in the spring.

Although the emphasis was now on farming, Dad set up a temporary office in the Loraine Hotel in Sumatra and kept regular office hours from 10 AM to 5 PM on Tuesdays and Fridays. Of course he was on call for emergencies at all times and he never refused to go when his services were needed regardless of weather, time of day, distance or how he might be feeling.

After moving from Hibbard to the ranch in 1915 we transferred our religious worship to the small church and Sunday School organization at Sumatra. As in many western small towns there were not enough Protestant people in the area to support the construction of a church edifice, so all services were held in the school house. Sunday School was held every Sunday morning at ten o'clock and church services once a month at eleven with Reverend Fulford coming up from Forsyth.

About a dozen of us teenagers organized and attended the Methodist young peoples' society known as the Epworth League. Later most of the Protestant women in the community organized a Ladies Aid Society of which Mother was president, guiding the group for its first three years. Meetings were held once a month from April until November, quite often in our home.

Dad was chosen superintendent of the Sunday School and occasionally he substituted for the preacher when Rev. Fulford or Rev. W. C. Smith were unable to make their regular visits. All in all, the Midgett family was extremely active in the Protestant services as well as supporting them to the extent of our financial abilities. Although money was often hard to come by, my parents never failed to tithe their income to the Methodist home and foreign missions.

Because the majority of the settlers in the Sumatra area were descendants of or direct emigrants from central Europe they were predominantly Roman Catholic. In 1915 they began construction on a new church with Fred Messmer as the contractor. Most of the labor was supplied by members of the faith, and within two years the building was ready for occupancy. It was given the name of St. Philomena, later changed to St. Isadora. The families of the congregation purchased their own pews as they were able, and since most of them had quite a few children they required a good few feet of seating space. The Catholic church was well attended and people drove in from as far as ten or fifteen miles to the services in good weather. During the first few years, their pulpit was filled by a traveling priest but by 1920 a priest was resident in Melstone, serving Sumatra and Ingomar.

The sturdiness of the church's construction is attested by the fact that sixty years later it still stands, is in good condition and services are occasionally held in it. A number of marriages have taken place there in recent years. Since the razing of the old Midgett house in 1973, the Catholic church now stands as the only original structure remaining on the town site.

*   *   *   *

Because my brother Bob would not be six until December 1, 1915, Betty and I were still the only Midgetts of school age. As long as the weather held we hitched old Cricket to the two wheeler cart every morning and drove in to Sumatra to school. The little mare was tied to the hitching rack north of the school building and given a few oats and some water at noon along with the other horses that had been ridden or driven to school. On days that Dad had office hours we rode in and out with him in the Model T.

Later in the winter, when the temperature dropped to zero or below, it was sometimes very difficult to start the car and our efforts to get it going involved some contortions. There were no patented anti-freeze solutions available in those days; the radiator was drained every night and refilled with hot water next morning. Often wads of paper were burned beneath the carburetor to vaporize the fuel and frequently one or two spark plugs were removed and small amounts of gasoline squirted directly into the cylinders. There were no electric starters until many years later so Dad and I often turned the hand crank over many times before the engine started and picked up enough speed to continue running. Little wonder we used to call it our "coffee grinder".

At times it was necessary to jack up the rear wheels to make the job easier by reducing the drag on the differential. All in all, it took a lot of back bending and elbow grease to make an automobile run in the cold weather. When all efforts failed, as they often did, Betty and I would saddle up Cricket and ride her double into town, leaving her at the livery stable while we were at school. If Dad succeeded in starting the car during the day he would come in and get us and we would trot the little mare home behind the car. Sometimes a week or more passed before we were able to use the old Tin Lizzie.

In the fall of 1915 we had late autumn rains giving the newly planted winter wheat a good start and leaving the soil and the reservoirs in fine shape for the winter freezeup. The water supply for the stock was ample for at least two or three months before we would have to haul it from the railroad tank car in Sumatra or the Adams' well one half mile south of our place.

As in Hibbard, good water for drinking and cooking purposes was scarce and most people living in the immediate vicinity of Sumatra depended on the water hauled in by the railroad from the Yellowstone River. We did not try to dig for water on our place as the Burnetts and Adams had good wells that they offered to share with us. Although the water was slightly alkaline it served the purpose and greatly reduced the job of having to haul it from town.

Except for crowded conditions in the school the year moved along smoothly. It was good to have Mrs. Adams as our teacher again. I have always felt my year in the eighth grade at Sumatra was one of my best and I learned more than in any other similar period. This was especially true of English, in which I learned much about grammar and sentence construction that I have never forgotten. Enrollment had increased to forty students with all eight grades represented and two of us expected to graduate in May—Opal Adams, and I.

Most of the kids were strangers to Betty and me at first but we soon added a host of new friends whom we came to know very well in the next few years. I saw my Hibbard girlfriend less and less often as the year went by. But, although there were quite a few cute girls in school, none seemed to attract my attention as Hazel had a year earlier. Perhaps I wasn't old enough yet to regard the boy-girl relationship as being one of the more important aspects of my life.

My greatest interest still lay in sports, taking after Dad, who had been quite proficient in his younger days. Baseball had been his forte and, while in medical school in Chicago from 1898 to 1902, he was offered a tryout as a catcher with the White Sox. He turned down their proposition for fear of ruining his hands, as he had hopes of becoming a surgeon. As a youngster I was encouraged by him to participate in sports and while still in Illinois I played quite a lot of baseball and tennis, the two most popular participation sports of the day. Basketball and football were still in their infancy and were just becoming popular as college and high school activities when we left the east.

*   *   *   *

Thanksgiving and Christmas gave us kids a welcome break in the school routine but very few people left the area during the holiday season. Mother invited Mrs. Adams, her three children, and the Morrises to our home for Thanksgiving dinner for which we had our first turkey since arriving in Montana. In turn, after opening our gifts at home Christmas morning, we were well entertained the rest of the day at the Adams home. The piece-de-resistance of the sumptuous meal was a big fat goose that our hosts had raised from a gosling. Other dinner guests were Charley and Grace Burnett, their three children, Clifford, Wilbur and Charlotte, and Grace's mother whom we all knew as Grandma Pratt.

During the afternoon Opal and Morris hitched up their driving team to a new cutter sleigh and the five oldest kids spent a couple of hours riding around the country. By the time we returned, Dad and Mom and the little ones had gone home to milk Daisy and feed the other stock. After I filled the wood box and the coal scuttles, Mom prepared a light lunch for us and we spent the rest of the evening examining our gifts and playing with our toys. When we finally hit the hay I am sure the folks were glad to see us all tucked in.

The weather that blew in with the New Year, 1916, was considerably colder during January and February than the year before. Heavy snows combined with high winds to pile drifts up around the house and farm buildings to heights of six feet or more. On many mornings we had to dig through knee-high snow to clear the path to the barn and the lane to the road before we could start for school. How everybody got around as well as they did is a mystery to me now. Maybe our world was not moving so fast and people were not in such a hurry to get places as they are today and this contributed to an entirely different concept of individual and social relationships.

The snow, banked up around most of the barn, helped to insulate the walls and keep the animals warmer during the cold weather that lasted well into March. It also provided a source of water for us and the animals. On warmer days we rode one of the horses and led Daisy and the other two horses the half mile down to the little reservoir where we kept a hole chopped in the ice from which water could be dipped for the livestock. This made a lot of additional work and we were glad when the first spring chinooks blew in from the southwest and the big drifts began to melt. Runoff was greater than it had been in 1915 so the water holes were well filled by the middle of May.

Despite the moisture from the melting snows, the crop and grass lands early in the growing season became much drier than during the previous spring. Although both the spring and winter wheat greened up nicely in May, growth slowed in June when late spring rains failed to materialize. Only cool weather saved the crop from burning up before the middle of July. A couple heavy showers later in the month helped the grain fill out and most of the farmers harvested fifteen to twenty-five bushels per acre.

Even with a smaller crop, wheat growers were as well or better off than they had been a year earlier for grain prices had increased considerably because of the war situation. No. 1 Turkey Red was bringing about $2.50 a bushel, and our crop of a little more than 1200 bushels was worth over $3,000 at harvest time. Dad stored more than five hundred bushels in the wooden bin he had built on the place in anticipation that prices would continue to rise.

*   *   *   *

During the 1915-16 winter a great deal of feeling had developed among the people living in the Sumatra school district in favor of building a new structure before the next term. With the graduation of two eighth graders at Sumatra and a few others expected from the surrounding rural schools, the need for a high school in the near future had become apparent. The closest ones at the time were at Forsyth and Roundup, fifty miles away. Plans were drawn up with the help of a Miles City architect and a bond election for $25,000 to raise the money for a four-room building with basement was passed by the voters in April 1916. The bonds were sold to a Miles City bank in May and construction started on the building early in June.

Excavation of the basement took only a few days, all done by horses and scoops, and when the excavation was completed more than eight hundred cubic yards of gumbo had been spread around a hole 70 by 50 feet and six feet deep. The plans provided for four classrooms, 25 by 40 feet, two on each floor, separated by a hall and stairway ten feet wide. A coal furnace in the basement supplied the hot air heating system. The ground floor rooms were to be used by the first six grades, three in the west room and the other three in the east room. The seventh and eighth grades were located in the west room upstairs and the east room was to be the high school. Because of the time factor, the school board had decided to try to complete only the two downstairs rooms for the coming school term and the upstairs was to be left until the spring of 1917.

By mid-July the foundation of the new school had been laid and construction of the framework was started. The Jones brothers and Fred Messmer had been hired by the contractor to supervise the job and three or four other local residents were also employed. By the first of August the studding and rafters had been raised and the rough siding had been applied one board at a time. There was no prefabrication in those days. Each board was sawed by hand to its required length and fastened together by hammer and nails. Slowly but steadily the big building took shape and by the first of September the chimney was up and roof was on. Weather was favorable for the workers and progress was rapid on the interior with the lathing and plastering completed before the floor was laid. The target date of October 15, set at the beginning of construction, was being met in every detail. By the first of October they were ready for the desks in the lower rooms and the installation of the hot air furnace. A primer coat of paint was applied to protect the fir siding from the winter rigors but the other two coats had to wait until spring.

After passing the state eighth grade examinations conducted by the county superintendent of schools in May 1916, I was determined to go on to high school in the fall. The folks agreed I should, but since construction of the new school had started so late it appeared I would have to leave home for my freshman year. This resulted in a couple of visits by Dad and me to Forsyth where I was enrolled. Arrangements were made for me to stay with the Frank Bland family where I was to pay thirty dollars a month for board and room. This was a tidy sum of money for my folks to spare at that time but, looking back, I didn't give it much thought then. I was quite excited about the prospective new experience, as I had never been away from home. Within a month Mrs. Bland's ill health made it necessary for me to leave and I moved across the alley and lived the rest of the year with the L.W. Wakefield family.

Even as these matters were transpiring, another development was taking place which had as much, if not more, effect on the Midgett family during the next few years. During the winter of 1915-16 Dad had been corresponding with his brother, Ross, who was a pharmacist in Blue Island, Illinois, a suburb of Chicago. Uncle Ross, as I knew him, had been ailing for about two years and recently his doctors had diagnosed his illness as tuberculosis and advised him to go someplace where the air was cleaner and dryer. The climate in Montana met those qualifications his first letter, received early in the winter, requested advice from Dad about the possibilities of coming to our part of Montana for a year or two at least. After three or four more letters passed between them, Dad decided to set up a combination office and drug store in Sumatra and Ross would be the pharmacist. At the time it seemed to be an ideal arrangement, and he had great hopes for the venture, even though it meant we would likely give up the farm if it turned out successfully.

Fortunately for Dad, the problem of setting up the store turned out to be much easier than any of us anticipated. With the new school under construction the town hall building was offered for sale and Dad's offer to purchase it was accepted. He bought a thirty foot lot on the east side of Main Street, and after excavating a basement and laying a foundation the building was hauled to the site, set up, and after some alterations, became a drug store.

The front of the building was remodeled to a facade with glass windows five feet high clear across it except for the door that was recessed about two feet in the center. By October 1916, shelving and cupboards had been built in, show cases had been moved into their places, and the first order of merchandise had been received from Minneapolis Drug Company. Uncle Ross and Aunt Florence and their pet poodle had arrived in early August and a small three-room house directly behind the store became their home for the winter.

The drug store was divided by partition about two-thirds of the way back, the front part containing show cases and most of the shelves on which the pharmaceutical and sundry items were displayed. In the back were the medicinal drugs and in the south east corner an eight by ten foot office was partitioned off to house Dad's desk and an examination table.

We had no electricity so a two-mantle gasoline lamp was hung from the ceiling above the main partition so it would light up the entire building. Every time we lit it we had to climb a ladder to take it down, fill it with gasoline and forced air, light it and then hang it back on its hook. The store was heated by a pot-bellied coal stove in the back that required constant firing in the winter to warm the store enough to keep liquid drugs and other articles from freezing at night. Often many items had to be covered even though the fire was banked the last thing at night and stoked again the first thing in the morning. Dad often had to go in at 10 o'clock on cold winter nights and again at five in the morning to keep the fires burning.

Because Uncle Ross knew the drugs better than the rest of us, it became his job to check original invoices, price the hundreds of items, and arrange them in the show cases and shelves. Everything was pretty well standardized as to price, and most retail prices allowed

TABLE II: THE PHARMACIST'S SHELF

1. Absorbine Jr.
2. Alcohol, Ethyl
3. Alcohol, Wood
4. Alka Seltzer
5. Analgesique Balm Ben Gue
6. Antiphlogistine
7. Asofoetida
8. Bayer Aspirin
9. Bell-Ans for Indigestion
10. Blue Vitriol (CuSO4)
11. Brilliantine Hair Oil
12. Bromo Seltzer
13. Calomel
14. Camphor
15. Carter's Little Liver Pills
16. Cascara Sagrada
17. Castile Soap
18. Castoria, Fletchers
19. Castor Oil
20. Chamberlains Liniment
21. Chloroform
22. Cigars - Roi Tans, Chancellors, Dutch Masters
23. Cigarettes - Camels, Chesterfields, Fatimas, Lucky Strikes, Old Golds, Sweet Caporals
24. Coca Cola
25. Cocoa Butter
26. Colgates Tooth Paste
27. Colgates Shaving Soap
28. Copenhagen Snuff
29. Cuticura Ointment
30. Cuticura Soap
31. Danderene Hair Dressing
32. Diamond Dyes
33. Doane's Pills
34. Dr. Kilmer's Swamp Root
36. Dr. Scholl's Zeno Pads
37. Dr. Scholl's Bunion Plasters
38. Epsom Salts
39. Ether
40. Ex-Lax
41. Foley's Honey & Tar
42. Freezone
43. Glycerin & Rose Water Lotion
44. Glyco-Thymoline
45. Gold Medal Harlem Oil
46. Hair Groom
47. Hall's Catarrh Medicine
48. Hershey's Chocolate
49. Hire's Root Beer
50. Hydrogen Peroxide
51. Ingersol Watches
52. Iodine
53. Ivory Soap
54. Jergens Lotion

TABLE II (cont.)

#	Item	#	Item
55.	Jergens Soap	79.	Noxzema Skin Cream
56.	Johnson & Johnson Adhesive Tape	80.	Nujol Lubricant
		81.	Nux Vomica
57.	Johnson & Johnson Bandages	82.	Palmolive Soap
		83.	Palmolive Shaving Cream
58.	Johnson & Johnson Cotton	84.	Parker's Hair Balsam
59.	Kodak Cameras & Films	85.	Pazo Hemorrhoidal Ointment
60.	Kremola Face Cream	86.	Pebeco Tooth Paste
61.	Lava Soap	87.	Pepsodent Tooth Paste
62.	Lavoris		
63.	LePage's Paste & Mucilage	88.	Pine Tar Cough Syrup
		89.	Phillips Milk of Magnesia
64.	Licorice Root & Powder	90.	Pomade Hair Dressing
65.	Listerine		
66.	Luden's Cough Drops	91.	Potassium Permanganate
67.	Lydia Pinkham's Remedy	92.	Putnam's Dyes
68.	Lysol	93.	Q-Ban Hair Color
69.	Maybelline Eye Shade	94.	Sal Hepatica
		95.	Sheaffers Pens & Pencils
70.	Mennen's Shaving Soap	96.	Shinola Shoe Polish
71.	Mennen's After Shave Powder	97.	Sloan's Liniment
		98.	Smith Brothers Cough Drops
72.	Mentholatum		
73.	Mercuric Oxide	99.	Spohn's Distemper Compound
74.	Mercurochrome		
75.	Morphine	100.	Stacomb
76.	Murine Eye Wash	101.	Sulphur Compound
77.	Mustard Powder	102.	Swan Soap
78.	Musterole		

for a 16 2/3 to 25 percent profit including transportation costs. The letters of our cost code were always placed on each item for sale. Those forming the code for numbers 1 to 0 were c-l-a-k-r-i-s-t-o-p so an article costing 30 cents was marked with the letters <u>ap</u> over the retail price. Shelving this first order of supplies was a big job, but with Aunt Florence's efficient help and the limited time Dad and I could spare, the task was completed in a few days. The Midgett Pharmacy opened for business in mid-November, 1916.

Many of the staples in stock then are still common articles on the shelves of today's drug stores. Some hundred or more of these are listed here to show the products that have stood the test of approximately seventy years. These, of course, would make up only a small percentage of the hundreds of pharmaceutical products we find on the druggists' shelves today.

It is worth noting that many of the pharmaceuticals we regard as essential for treatment of our many ailments today, particularly the antibiotics, antihistamines, decongestants, vaccines, and sulfanilamides, are not in this list. It gives us some idea how greatly the medics of those days were handicapped in comparison with our modern specialists, clinics and hospitals. Dad depended on the old reliables such as aspirin, calomel, quinine, Epsom salts, and quarts and quarts of liniment, ointments, iodine, Antiphlogistine, castor oil, and hydrogen peroxide.

*   *   *   *

Mrs. Adams announced before the 1915-16 term of school was out that she was giving up teaching and would spend all of her time running her farm with the help of her son, Morris, and her brother, Hubert. The latter did a great deal of work on our place that summer helping Dad harvest the crop and seeding the winter wheat for the 1917 season. Threshing time was about the same as the previous year except we were able to feed the crew at our own place. A year older and ten pounds heavier I was more able to hold up my end of the job and was promoted from a spiker to stacker on the bundle wagons, from which I fed the bundles into the threshing machine.

One incident added to the excitement of the summer of 1916. Mrs. Adams had leased 80 acres of Section 19 to the west of her place and had planted corn on part of it for feed for her cows and horses. In late July she hired me to help Morris cut the weeds, mostly Russian thistles, out of the corn field. These were the "dog days" for rattlesnakes, a time when they shed their old skins, could not see or hear well and spent most of their daylight hours inactive in the shade of the thistles. One very hot, dry day Morris and I were moving up and down the rows chopping out the thistles when suddenly he let out a blood curdling yell and I jumped at least ten feet. Turning, I saw him pointing at a weed I had just cut out. Under it a large rattlesnake had coiled and was poised to strike at the nearest moving object—which happened to be me. Both of us reacted simultaneously raising our hoes and chopping the striking serpent cutting it into a dozen writhing pieces, one of which had eight or ten rattles. From then on we were a little more careful about how we passed up our deaf and sightless, but deadly friends. During the three days we spent in the corn patch we killed more than a dozen of them.

About the middle of June 1916, the county superintendent of schools, Miss Fay Alderson, made a public statement that she would not be a candidate for the office again. Dad and some of the local citizens interested in their children's education talked to Mrs. Adams and urged her to run in the August primary. She consented and easily won her party nomination. After a spirited campaign she was elected to the office in the November general election. She left the farm to Hubert and Morris in December and moved to Forsyth, the county seat where she held the office of superintendent for the next twelve years. Her daughter, Argin, was appointed her office assistant and her younger daughter, Opal, graduated from high school in Forsyth in 1920. Morris stayed on the farm for a number of years and he and his mother and sisters visited back and forth quite often.

*   *   *   *

Because I was away at school in Forsyth during the 1916-17 term, my memory is hazy about the details of the events in Sumatra from September to May. However, by Christmas Dad had decided he could not farm, run a drug store, and serve the medical needs of the area at the same time. He had been appointed railroad physician by the Milwaukee railroad and was granted a pass to ride anywhere on the system, and all the members of the family were given the same privilege. Twice a month Dad would send me the pass to come home from Forsyth for the weekend on Friday night on No. 17 and back on No. 18 Monday morning. The folks still lived at the ranch and I was never sure whether anyone would meet me or I would have to stay all night at one of the little hotels. Dad had a standing arrangement for a room for me if he couldn't come in but I often walked the two miles out to the ranch on moonlit nights when the weather was good. It was a little spooky sometimes when coyotes hunting cottontails or field mice suddenly let loose with their long eerie wails.

I was glad when Christmas vacation came and I could spend a few days at home. Although I had very little spending money, I managed to get a little Christmas gift for each of the other five members of the family. For Mother I got a package of gray celluloid hair pins. Her hair had begun to gray about the time I was born and by her early thirties it was completely silver in color. A tear appeared in her eye when she opened the tiny package and even though I was fourteen years old, I felt a great deal of pride in myself in bringing a little pleasure to my family. We were a close-knit family and the Christmas season always helped to bring us even closer together.

Plans for a third new house were in various stages of development each time I came home. By spring a very definite decision had been made to move into Sumatra as soon as possible. The most important factor in resolving the problem was the health of Uncle Ross. His condition had shown no improvement during his first few months in Montana and it was evident to Dad and Aunt Florence that his illness would be terminal, probably by spring. The long cold winter proved to be too much and by Christmas he had a very bad cough and considerable hemorrhaging of his lungs and trachea. He gradually lost weight and the strength to do any work at all. Aunt Florence tried to keep the store open with what help Dad could give her. On the 16th of April my uncle passed away. After a brief memorial service two days later, Aunt Florence accompanied his body by train back to Blue Island where he was buried in the city cemetery.

Although a month late opening in the fall of 1916, the school year in the new Sumatra school began with a total enrollment of over sixty-five pupils in the eight grades and two girls, Opal Adams and Gladys Williams in the freshman year of high school. Two grade teachers had been hired—Miss Maureen Olmstead, for the four lower grades and Miss Helen Holmes, a young local woman, for the upper grades. Two instructors, Mr. and Mrs. Niles H. Davis, were hired to teach the four subjects, English I, Algebra I, World History and Latin I, offered that first year to the high school students. Mr. Davis was also principal of the whole system.

Since the upstairs rooms were not finished, the two high school girls used Mr. Davis' office for a classroom and did their studying in the upper grade room. After Opal Adams went to Forsyth with her mother at Christmas time, Gladys was the only high school student for the remainder of the year. Others had been expected when school opened but when the building was not completed a few of them, like me, went to other schools. Elizabeth Schleder enrolled in the Catholic high school in Miles City.

While in Forsyth, I took the same four subjects mentioned above that made up the freshman year of what was commonly known as the Classical or College Entrance Course. Although neither one of my parents had ever put any pressure on me as to my future occupation, I believe Dad would have liked to see me follow his footsteps into the medical profession. I am also sure Mother would have been pleased if I had shown some inclination toward the ministry. At least we were all agreed that regardless of my choice, I was to go on to college upon graduation from high school.

In addition to the four basic college entrance courses, I also took manual training two days a week and a penmanship course once a week. Away from home and without much supervision, I think I surprised my folks at the end of the year when my final grade card showed I had a B average. I liked all my subjects but found algebra, the most difficult and had to be content with a C+ in it. I finished up with an A in Latin and really felt I excelled in the subject when the teacher called on me frequently to do work at the blackboard. I don't know my handwriting ever improved a great deal, and I never did become an accomplished carpenter as a result of taking manual training. In fact, these classes in Forsyth High School were the only opportunities I ever had to learn about these two subjects since the high school in Sumatra never became large enough to warrant the hiring of sufficient teaching staff to handle any frill subjects or extra-curricular work while I was still in school.

Chapter VI

Although little definitive information appears to have been written about the expanse of land between the lower Musselshell and Yellowstone rivers south of the Missouri, that which is available indicates that the more than 18,000 square miles of present day Garfield, Rosebud, McCone, Custer, Dawson, and Richland counties were favorite summer feeding grounds for millions of the buffalo that roamed the western high plains during the greater part of the nineteenth century. Even though this entire area was a part of the "Great American Desert" its lavish growth of Montana purple bunch grass with its highly nutritious qualities attracted great herds of the big shaggy beasts on their journeys through the plains east of the Rockies.

For many years after their disappearance there remained much tell-tale evidence in the form of their deep and narrow trails and the bleached bones of myriad animals slain by both the white and red inhabitants of this great open space. The water holes along the entire length of the big Porcupine, Muggins, Froze-To-Death, Blacktail, Breed, and Rattlesnake creeks slaked the thirst of the ambling creatures as they moved northward from the broad valley of the Yellowstone River on their way to the Musselshell and Missouri. Such a route undoubtedly placed hundreds of buffalo exactly on the Sumatra town site frequently during the 1860s and 1870s. Sources indicate this area was the destination of Indian tribes from both slopes of the Rockies who undertook annual hunts for buffalo as a source of food, clothing and shelter. The official report of the National Museum written by William Hornaday in 1887 describes the last official government buffalo hunt the previous year. A sketch map accompanying the report shows that the last wild buffalo in the U.S. was slain by a hunter, James McNaney, near the Buffalo Buttes which are shown on the map a few miles northeast of the Sumatra townsite.

During the next fifteen or twenty years when thousands of cattle were driven northward from Texas and other southwestern states over the Chisholm Trail and others to the west, many of the large herds ended up in the Big Dry country, 75 or 80 miles northeast of Sumatra. Others established permanent headquarters on Flatwillow Creek west of the Musselshell. In both instances some of these herds probably followed the old buffalo trails through western Rosebud County and the Sumatra country.

After the buffalo had disappeared from the plains and the great cattle drives had lost their impetus eastern Montana became a mosaic of overlapping cattle ranches with very poorly defined boundary lines. Due to the openness of the prairies, most ranchers ran as many as three or four large herds wherever there were ample native grasses to feed them. Often this took them a hundred miles or more from the home ranch. Thus, the area around Sumatra became grazing country for cattle whose winter homes were located as far away as Miles City (Fort Keogh) and Lewistown (Fort Maginnis). Because of frequent confusion of ownership among the herds, minor feuds developed but usually they were quickly settled without resort to bloodshed.

During the first decades of the 20th century much of the arable land was turned under by the plows of the new settlers as thousands of acres of the grazing land were planted to wheat. Barbed wire fences enclosed hundreds of quarter and half sections and the large open ranges became memories of the past. A few of the big ranches in eastern Montana that either went out of business or were broken up into smaller farming units following the blizzards of 1886-87 were the NH, NV, KBar, LU, STV, N, CK, XIT and the 79. By 1907 even the largest of them, including the Mill Iron, the Turkey Track, the Hashknife, the CY and the 3T spreads had shrunk to a fraction of their greatest expanse.

The development of the sheep industry in eastern Montana followed the decline of the big cattle ranches. From 1910, the woolies played an increasingly important part in the history of western Rosebud County. Despite the reduction of grazing space the sheep business flourished and the flocks increased in number and size. At least a half dozen camp wagons, each with a solitary herder and his dogs, could be seen on the hills a few miles from Sumatra on any given day from late March to November.

*   *   *   *

No element of uniqueness or extraordinary circumstance can be claimed for the founding and development of the little village of Sumatra. It was neither the locale of an accidental discovery of a few shiny flakes of precious metal nor was it an abandoned military post established for the protection of early settlers from Indians or to guard those intrepid surveyors and laborers who laid the rails of the Northern Pacific from the central plains to the Pacific coast. Nor did it owe its beginnings to its position as a marketing center of a once prosperous cattle-raising region. It did not have the good fortune to be located in the right place to be chosen by the railroad for a division terminus. It was not the head of navigation of one of the larger Montana rivers where traders brought their wares and many early settlers arrived and moved on into the fertile valleys of the northern and central portions of the state.

No—Sumatra was never fortunate enough to have any of these or other stimuli to live and grow—nothing but the deep faith, intense desire, and perseverance of a small, undaunted group of early settlers who believed there were good reasons for its existence and were willing to make sacrifices and pay the price necessary to develop a pleasant and viable place in which to live and raise their families.

As a matter of fact, the origin of the town can be easily explained, for it closely conformed to the pattern established by scores of little villages that sprang up in the settling of the west. One of the most important factors in the development of eastern Montana, especially this particular area, was the construction of the Milwaukee Railroad (C.M.St.P.&P.R.R.) from the Yellowstone Valley northwestward through the central part of the state.

For track maintenance the right-of-way was divided into sections about ten miles in length with a crew of two or more workers stationed at the center of each section. It was at these locations where little towns began to grow with the construction of a section house, a depot, and a warehouse to handle the many carloads of freight anticipated as the new settlers began to occupy the land opened up by the expanded Homestead Acts of 1909 and 1912.

Shortly after the completion of its trackage, the railroad company purchased land for town sites, laid them out in streets and lots, and offered the latter at very low cost to encourage development of a business community and home building for new settlers. The Sumatra site was located in the southeast quarter of Section 15, Township 10 North, Range 33 East and lots were platted on both sides of the railroad that ran in a southeast-northwest direction through the town.

The name for the town site is a subject that seems to defy explanation. So far as I know there was no outstanding early settler of this area whose name might have been given to this little town as in many places throughout the state. Neither was the name of the former home of one of these same newcomers bestowed on this little village.

The explanation that seems to have most credence is based upon topography, the town site being at the highest point on the railroad between the Yellowstone and the upper Musselshell valley. In other words, the town was located on a "summit" that became its original designation. However, this name was already in use by a small hamlet on top of the Rockies south of Glacier Park, a situation that necessitated the corruption of the name to "Sumatra," which it has remained for more than eighty years.

The first buildings in Sumatra were two railroad cars set off north of the tracks just east of Main Street in 1910 or 1911. One was used as a depot and freight house and the other housed the agent, Jess Hayes, and his wife, Wally. The original post office for the Sumatra area was set up in the depot with the agent as temporary postmaster. Two years later it was moved to the Mercantile, the second general store, and Elsie Gray became the first official postmistress. When the Imhoff-Carlen store was built in 1915 the post office was transferred to it and Dick Imhoff was appointed to run it. He hired George Bartlett as his assistant and a year later George took over as the fourth postmaster in five years. He continued in that job until 1919.

Sometime late in 1911 the railroad cars were replaced by the construction of a depot a few feet to the east and a house for the agent to the west across Main Street. The former was approximately 100 by 30 feet and was divided into three sections: a large 30 by 20 foot waiting room on the west, the ticket office and operator's counter in the middle, and the freight and express warehouse on the east end.

The agent's home, a one-story structure, contained a living room, two bedrooms, and a combination kitchen and dining room, but, as usual, was not equipped with the comforts of indoor plumbing. At the same time a section house was built behind and to the east of the depot and a big cylindrical tank to provide water for the railroad engines was erected adjacent to the track about 100 feet east of the warehouse. Water was pumped into the big tank from the reservoirs east and west of town.

About the same time the business section of the budding village began to develop with the construction of four buildings north of the railroad. The Fleetwood Hotel and the Midland Coal and Lumber Company with a 200 foot frontage, arose directly across Main Street from each other and the first general store soon followed a half block further north on the west side of the street. The builder of the hotel was a Mr. McDonald, land agent for the railroad, who soon sold it to some people named King who ran it for a few years when it was commonly known as "The Green Onion" because of its color. Harry Jaffe, one of the few Jews to settle in this part of Montana, was the builder and proprietor of the store. He also probably constructed the first family residence in Sumatra about two blocks north of the railroad and a block east of Main Street. The fourth commercial structure was a 100 foot high elevator built by the Yellowstone Elevator Co. to take care of the bountiful grain crops being produced by the homesteaders of these early years.

By 1913 the need for many other kinds of business had developed rapidly and Main Street began to take on the appearance of a town. A second hotel, the Loraine, was started next door north of the Fleetwood, a second general store, the Mercantile, and the one and only saloon the town ever had soon went up between the Mercantile and the Jaffe store. The hotel was built by the Carmichael brothers as was the livery stable behind it and both were managed by the Bruce Hayes family for the next few years. Henry Enger, who also had a store in Ingomar, built and managed the Mercantile but sold it to Walt Swinney, an employee, within a year or so. W.E.(Cotton) Duff built and ran the saloon until prohibition became the law after the Volstead Act was passed by Congress. The most imposing business building in Sumatra was erected in 1914 when the Californians, Imhoff and Carlen, bought two lots north of and across the street from the bank location. The store stocked the largest quantity and variety of merchandise of the three general stores.

Accompanying the increase of business in the area was the need for an institution for the safe-keeping and exchange of all the money the wheat farmers expected from their abundant crops. This need was more than adequately satisfied when late in 1913 the firm of Wiley, Clark and Greening established one of its numerous small banks in Sumatra. It occupied the only brick building ever constructed in the town and was located at the north end of the Jaffe block. Its manager was Robert Ross, a very affable and competent young fellow who received his training for the job as an employee of the company's bank in Miles City.

The first and only garage in Sumatra until the mid 1920s was originally a blacksmith and repair shop. Its main business was shoeing hundreds of work and saddle horses, repairing farm machinery, wagons, and buggies, and sharpening plowshares that lost their edges quickly in the rocky soil of the area. By 1916 it had been mostly converted into a car repair shop for the Model T's and other autos making their appearance in increasing numbers. Over the garage, a block north of the bank, were six or eight rooms, four of which were occupied by the owners, Harvey and Cora Bartlett. The others were rented to teachers and other newcomers to the community.

A weekly newspaper, the *Sumatra Record*, was printed in late 1912 in Forsyth by Jack McCausland, the editor and publisher of the *Rosebud County Record*. Early in 1914 Henry Polk and his wife came from Missouri with their hand-operated printing press and other equipment, bought out Mr. McCausland, and set up their shop on a lot just north of the garage.

The Yellowstone Lumber Company bought the west half of the Jaffe block and set up a general building supply business. It was generally believed that Harry Jaffe originally owned the entire block where his store was located as well as quite a few additional well-selected lots in the downtown section. These lots were purchased for the bank and other business houses along Main Street.

Beyond the print shop was the town hall that was used as a school house for about four years before the new four-room building northwest of the downtown area was constructed in 1916. Late in the same year the town hall was moved south and across the street and converted into the Midgett Pharmacy. The only other business buildings were Jack Buchanan's blacksmith shop, the Jaffe warehouse, and a third lumber yard, all on the street a block east of Main Street. No other buildings were erected north of the drug store on the east side of the street until well into the 1920s.

One entire block directly east of the bank and north of the drug store was purposely left vacant. Plans for a city park there never materialized, probably due to the lack of enough water to irrigate the trees and grass. A much more appropriate site for such a project would have been the west shore of the East Lake which was formed by the railroad embankment and in which springs provided an ample supply of water year round.

*   *   *   *

During the warmer months the sixty-foot wide Main Street was either a sea of sticky gumbo when wet or two to four inches of heavy gray dust after drying out in the hot summer sun and wind. Since there were no cross walks it was a very difficult to get from one side of the street to the other on foot through the gooey gumbo in the wet weather. Although it was improved a little by spreading ashes and gravel in the right places, the coating was usually washed away by a heavy rain.

One incident comes to mind that illustrates this situation. Little Johnny Bonser, about five years old, lived with his folks in one of the hotels. He spent his time during the day running from one store to the next begging for candy. One day early in the summer a heavy downpour left Main Street a quagmire. An hour or so after the rain Dad and I looked out the store front window and there was little Johnny wading across the muddy street. Arriving at the porch he climbed up on it covered with gumbo from head to foot. Striding up to Dad he pointed down to his feet and, with a big grin covering his face, said "I got stuck in the mud and I lost my shroes but I didn't lose my shrockins." He had made our day but I heard later his mother did not enjoy it quite as much as we had.

It was not until 1917 or 18 that the new state highway was built on the north side of the railroad from Bascom to Sumatra. Here it crossed back to the south side and for the first time Main Street was greatly improved by a new gravel surface three or four inches deep. The other streets of the little town remained in much the same condition as when the town site was originally laid out—graded dirt with a very thin mixture of natural gravel that helped little during the wet weather.

Both sides of Main Street were bordered by five-foot-wide wooden sidewalks that, in front of the saloon and the new store, were expanded into porches about eight feet wide. Dad also built a porch across the front of the drug store where we kept the empty ice cream kegs before shipping them back to the Miles City Creamery. The decor of Main Street was completed by hitching racks in front of the Mercantile and the saloon, and along the south side of the Imhoff-Carlen store. From 1917 on, the need for these racks gradually lessened as the automobile became more and more common, and horses as a means of transportation faded from the picture. By 1920 the racks were things of the past, only a memory of earlier days.

In 1916 the residential section of Sumatra consisted of roughly 30 homes scattered over approximately ten to twelve of the twenty blocks in the part of the town site north of the tracks. No residences were ever constructed south of the tracks. There was no natural arboreal growth or grass suitable for lawns, although many attempts were made by the town's residents to grow shelter belts and produce good sod for their yards. Very few were successful as the trees and grass either dried up in the hot arid summer weather or froze out in

PHOTOS

Dr. J.E. Midgett and friend, first visit to Montana, 1913

Dr. Midgett and Cricket on rounds

Sumatra, looking west from the water tower

Main Street: looking north (top); looking south (bottom)

Looking south

R.C. Church, Dormitory, School

Business district, looking south

Residences

The "Ranch"

The "Baby House"

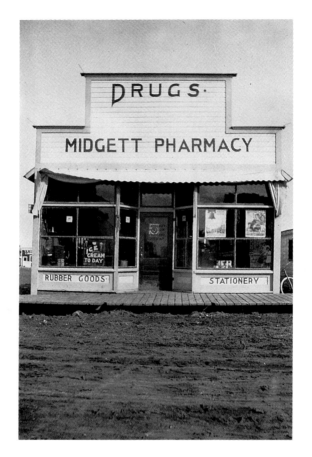

Midgett Pharmacy

Sumatra RR station

School

4th of July, parade and celebration (Betty Midgett on horseback)

Dr. Midgett in his wheatfield during the good years

The Midgett family, pre-Phyllis

Sumatra schoolchildren, grades 1-12

Schoolchildren at depot, waiting for a troop train during World War I

You are cordially invited to attend the
Graduating Exercises
Sumatra High School
on Friday evening, May the twenty-first
Nineteen hundred twenty
Sumatra Hall

Class Roll

GLADYS L. WILLIAMS ELIZABETH R. SCHLEDER
J. KENT MIDGETT

Class Motto
TO THE STARS THRU DIFFICULTY

Class Colors **Class Flower**
PURPLE AND GOLD PINK CARNATION

Sumatra High School, first graduating class

The author as High School graduate

Epworth League at Neihart, 1922—Methodists at play

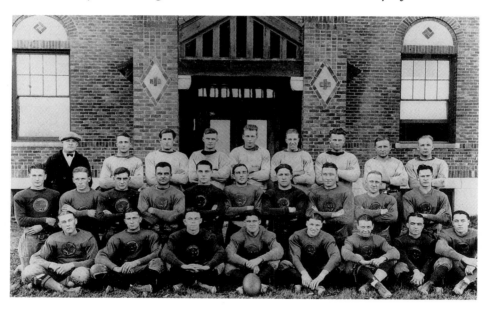

Montana Wesleyan football team, early 1920s—Methodists in uniform
The 129 lb. behemoth—4th from left, back row

the five-month winters. During the good years from 1912 to 1918 most families raised quite ample gardens but there was no way to augment nature's meager supply of precipitation during the summer except by carrying or pumping water from a well or the nearest pond or reservoir. This task took many hours of Dad's and my time, his in the early morning when he was up by five o'clock nearly every day to do his chores before breakfast. My brother, Bob, nearly eight years old in 1917, helped me in the evenings to haul water on a two-wheeled cart the 200 yards up hill from the East Lake in two ten gallon cans. Mother tried to raise a few shrubs and flowers around the house but was never very successful.

When we arrived in Montana in 1914 most of the homestead land had been taken up and fenced by three strands of barbed wire. Most roads in the area followed the section lines with many short cuts angling across unfenced railroad sections that had not yet been settled. As the years passed many of these trails were obstructed by barbed wire and the main roads graded and graveled by the county. Many others were eventually abandoned and covered over by natural growth of sage brush, buffalo grass and Russian thistles, more commonly known as tumbleweeds because of their tendency to roll across the prairies after ripening. After a few years most of these roads and trails were completely obliterated with only dim ruts to indicate where they had been.

The town population of Sumatra consisted of families whose heads were predominantly male in those days. Very few women worked away from home except schoolteachers and nurses, so most members of the gentler sex in this little town were busy caring for their own families. There was little need for baby-sitters since there were few places to go. Usually the families were large enough that the older children could look after the younger ones when Papa and Mamma occasionally went out for the evening.

By the time the U.S. entered World War I several occupations were represented among the residents of Sumatra. The railroad offered an assortment of jobs and at least ten people were employed in such diverse positions as section foreman, laborers, water pumper, telegraph operators, ticket agents, freight hustlers and carpenters.

On Main Street the signs indicated a wide variety of other types of work: hotel keepers, restaurant owners, waitresses, cooks, store owners, clerks, livery stable manager, saloon keeper, barber, bank manager, bookkeeper, cashier, and other bank employees, newspaper publisher, grain elevator operator, drayman, oil wholesaler, fuel dealer, farm implement dealer, car salesman, druggist, doctor, postmaster, and finally, teachers and others connected with the school.

Although this seems a rather extensive list of occupations, there were many not represented in the little town during this period. We had no lawyer, dentist, clergyman, mortician, jeweler, beauty operator, accountant, photographer, insurance agent, architect, realtor, veterinarian, optometrist, plumber, electrician, garbage collector, telephone installer and operator, dry cleaner and laundry operator. Any of the latter services could be procured only by correspondence or making the 50-mile trip to Forsyth or Roundup. Anyone who might have been engaged in one of these pursuits would probably have starved in Sumatra as there was not sufficient demand for his services to make a decent living.

*   *   *   *

North of Sumatra in the area known as the "Breaks of the Missouri" many ranches had already been established by the time further revisions in the Homestead Act were passed by Congress in 1912. Some of these settlers were descendants of the original cattle ranchers who had "squatted" on some of the best range land south of the Missouri River and east of the Musselshell. Numerous small tributaries of these two streams provided ample supplies of water for thousands of cattle, and the lush native grasses of the region produced top weight animals within three or four years.

Since this area was nearly 100 miles from railroad shipping before the Milwaukee Road extended its rails west of Miles City, it continued as cattle country even after most of the land nearer the tracks had been turned over and sowed to wheat and other small grains. Elevators were too far away and road conditions too risky most of the year to make farming profitable in the hinterlands even when crop yields were good. Most years wild hay harvest from the many broad creek valleys was more than ample to feed the livestock over the long cold winters when two to three feet of snow covered the range.

A most difficult problem in these remote areas was transportation, particularly the delivery of mail and parcels. Before the Milwaukee arrived postal service to the "North Country" was directed via the Great Northern Railroad and transferred at Glasgow and some other stations on the hi-line. From there it was ferried across the Missouri River to rural post offices that had been established at Haxby, Butte Creek, Brusett and two or three other places south of the river. A few others such as Edwards and Sand Springs were serviced by the Northern Pacific Railroad from Miles City via Jordan, a distance of nearly 120 miles. Settlers living in the vicinity of these small distribution points traveled by horseback in summer or sled in winter to pick up their letters and packages along with a few staple groceries the postmaster or mistress stocked in small amounts.

The coming of the railroad to Sumatra and establishment of a Post Office made a very important change in the mail situation for these isolated people. Long time-consuming round trips from Miles City and Glasgow were reduced by almost two thirds in time and distance, and undependable ferries across the Missouri were eliminated. The little community of Sand Springs was now only forty miles north of the Sumatra station and its post office, and thus became the distributing center for the numerous branch offices, many of which were located in the ranch homes scattered over the wide expanse of the territory. Between twelve and fifteen of these small offices existed at some time between 1910 and 1920. In addition to those mentioned above these included Brunelds, Bruce, Snowbelt, Alice, McTwiggan, Benzien, Dilo, Bowmanville, Anad, Tindall, and two or three others whose names I no longer recall.

All mail addressed to these little post offices was sorted by postal employees on the Milwaukee trains and dropped off at the Sumatra depot. Only first class mail was carried on Trains 15 and 16 and it was thrown off about 200 feet west of the depot while they rushed by at a speed of 15 to 40 miles per hour. The outgoing mail sack was hung on a collapsible crane near the track and picked off by a large hook contraption as it passed rapidly by. Trains 17 and 18 stopped at all the stations so all classes of mail were unloaded on the depot platform. It was the postmaster's job to get it to the post office and most of the time it was hauled in a small two-wheeled cart. During the summers of 1919 and 1920 I had the task of transporting the mail to and from the post office and hanging it for the two fast trains to pick up. It was always a mystery to me that the heavy canvas and leather mail bags were not ripped in pieces when the big hook grabbed them from the crane but I don't remember it ever happening.

After mail was delivered to the post office that addressed to the "North Country" was resacked into separate bags hanging from a partitioned rack occupying nearly half the floor space of the Sumatra post office. Up to about 1916 or 1917 the sacks were loaded into a four-horse-drawn freight wagon that started on its twice a week, 40-mile trip to Sand Springs and back. In nice weather the round trip could easily be made in two days, but in wet or snowy weather it often took two days each way with an overnight stop at Snowbelt, about half-way.

On the return trip outgoing mail from the rural post offices was picked up at Sand Springs and delivered to Sumatra where it was sorted, sacked for points east, west, north and south, and loaded on the Milwaukee trains. It was not until 1917 that motorized vehicles were adopted for delivery and the number of trips north was increased to three per week. At the same time the road was improved by grading and gravelling and most of the time the trip could be made in one day. In a couple of years the fifteen or more little post offices had been reduced to five or six.

*   *   *   *

Henry Kreider was a big rawboned young fellow barely in his twenties whose Herculean efforts and willingness to help others made it possible for scores of people to make safe journeys to the north country and hundreds of others to receive mail on time despite muddy roads and unfavorable weather. Hank was a young German who had filed on a homestead in the Sand Springs area and had bid in the mail-carrying contract when it was offered by the P.O. Department in 1914 or 1915.

Big Hank picked up the freight and express for the little stores up north in the evening and early next morning loaded orders of groceries and other commodities for settlers along the route. He always saved plenty of space for the sacks of mail and parcel post that went on last. At least once a week he had a passenger or two who had arrived on one of the four trains on their way to the hinterland.

Many interesting stories came from the experiences of Hank and his passengers on what later became the Sand Springs Stage. One adventure, that took place in the summer of 1916, a year or so before Henry motorized his outfit by buying a Ford model T truck, was the most exasperating for those involved and amusing to those who learned about it later.

One Monday morning in early August the four-horse team pulled out of town with the usual heavy load that had accumulated over the three day weekend. Two lady passengers from the east had arrived the night before on No. 17 and Henry had picked them up at the Loraine Hotel. The first ten miles were uneventful and progress was made to within a couple of miles of Sage Creek when disaster struck. About midnight, twelve hours earlier, a typical Montana cloudburst had struck from the northwest and three or four of the creeks running into the Musselshell were running bank full through the north country. The heavy gumbo roads were soaked, and as Hank and his loaded wagon approached the creek's crossing the iron wheels sank deeper and deeper into the mud. An 18-inch culvert usually handled the heavy flow of water from snow runoff and rains that hit the area, but this time it was different. The cloudburst had been so sudden and the torrent of water rushing down the gully so massive it had washed out the culvert and created a channel six to eight feet deep and twelve to fifteen feet wide.

As they topped the low rise leading down to the creek a very discouraging sight that met the eyes of the three people perched upon the two spring seats of the big triple-paneled wagon. It was not the first time Hank had seen a washout but he quickly perceived that this was the worst one. After slipping and sliding the last hundred yards down the slope he stepped on the foot brake with all of his 190 pounds and pulled the big team to the left at the same time.

A disaster was averted when the wagon came to rest about ten feet from the cutbank that had been eroded away by the rushing water. After a couple of deep breaths, Hank jumped to the ground to help his badly frightened passengers from their perches. Since it was now past noon on a hot day the three decided to take time off to eat the lunches that had been put up for them at the hotel. Henry unhitched the horses and led them further down the creek where they could get a drink. The ladies found a shady place under a cottonwood and spread out the food while the horses were being fed a nourishing mixture of corn and oats.

Lunch over, the next job was to figure out how to get the big load across the creek. While they were eating three two-horse rigs, one from the south and two from the north, made timely arrivals on the scene. Lightly loaded, they experienced little difficulty crossing downstream a hundred yards from the washed-out road, but it didn't go so well for Henry when he tried to drive through at the same spot. Halfway across the big rear wheels dropped off a rocky ledge and settled nearly hub deep into a sandy layer that seemed to have no bottom. The harder the horses pulled, the deeper the wagon sank until it sat on the bottom of the pool. Finally, after coaxing, swearing, and slapping of lines resulted in no further progress, Hank decided there must be some other way.

Stuck smack in the middle of the stream there was only one thing left to do—start unloading. Since the women had gone on across on one of the other conveyances, the first and probably most important part of the load to move was Uncle Sam's mail—all 200 pounds of it. Four or five more tugs but nothing moved. Next to come out were the 400 or 500 pounds of groceries and other supplies ordered and picked up at the three general stores. Another series of pulls—another failure to move the wagon and the remaining contents. This continued until the wagon was empty, but still no results. As a last resort the wagon box was removed from the running gear and floated the twenty feet across the creek. Hank then grabbed the lines, gave the horses a resounding slap across their rumps, sounded a loud ear-piercing yell and, lo and behold, a miracle—the wheels turned and the wagon crossed the shallow water to dry land.

Since the numerous articles emptied from the wagon had already been carried or hauled across the creek by the three helpful neighbors and others who had arrived in the meantime, it was a comparatively easy job to replace the wagon box and reload its cargo. By late afternoon Henry and his friends were on their way to the halfway station where they arrived a few hours later to stay overnight and relax from the adventure.

*   *   *   *

The location of Sumatra as the northernmost station on the Milwaukee through Rosebud County had turned out to be its greatest asset when, by 1910, it became the nearest shipping point for this vast country to the north. An average of two or three "immigrant cars" a week brought in the livestock, household furnishings, and other belongings of the new settlers. Most of the freight and supplies for the area were shipped into Sumatra for transportation by wagon train to outlying points.

By 1916 the volume of freight and express received at the Sumatra depot had increased to such an extent that the railroad doubled the capacity of its warehouse. From 1911 and 1915 it was a common occurrence to see eight or ten freight wagons a day with six or eight horses each headed northward loaded with lumber, fence posts, barbed wire, building supplies, furniture, groceries, and other supplies for the new homes and small general stores scattered throughout the area. A couple of years later, with the coming of motorized transportation, trucks replaced the bay and gray quadrupeds and time for the trip was cut in half.

The difficulty of transportation was closely related to and affected by another equally important but even less developed service, that of communications. Even the original dwellers of the region were better off with their smoke signals and other means of contacting their neighbors than were the settlers of the early 1900's.

The inventions of Edison, Bell, and Marconi had been in use by the general public of the U.S. for many years but they remained unavailable in most of the thinly populated rural areas of eastern Montana when my folks lived there.

Because of the sparse population and the distance between settlements the few telephone systems in eastern Montana in 1915 had not found it profitable to extend their facilities beyond the more populous towns, leaving rural regions without service of any kind. Other than a few lines that neighboring ranchers strung along the fence rows between their places, most settlers were entirely dependent upon their fastest means of transportation for effective communication. As late as 1915 or 1916 this was a good saddle horse ridden at a pace of ten or twelve miles per hour on routes that cut across sections instead of going the long way around on the road.

Many calls my Dad received for medical services were of this nature and he often answered them the same way. Beginning in 1916 the dependable steed was increasingly replaced by the Model T and other motor cars rapidly coming on the market. The telephone was a missing quantity in that area for the next fifty years and it wasn't until 1973 that service was extended to the few families living there.

Other communication media such as radio and television were also slowly available to the people of Sumatra and vicinity because of the distance from transmitting centers. By 1925 no more than a half dozen low-power broadcasting stations had been set up east of the Montana Rockies, each one transmitting less than a hundred miles. It was almost another quarter of a century before television became available to most of Montana and it wasn't until the 1960's that the few people left around Sumatra enjoyed good reception. So, the lack of good communication has been one of the area's most serious problems since the beginnings of homestead days.

*   *   *   *

In the final analysis the development of any country depends on one very important factor, the composition and fertility of its soil. This is especially true in regions where there are no natural mineral resources or primal forest areas capable of producing timber of commercial value and quantity. Such was the case in the greater part of eastern Montana in the early 1900's when it was being settled by arrivals from east and west who had been conned into believing that good living could easily be had merely by filing on 320 acres of the abundant land opened up by the passage of the Homestead Acts.

In Rosebud County and the Sumatra territory there was little to stimulate development and sustain a population except the productivity of the soil, either to raise grain crops or livestock. Except for small, widely scattered pockets of coal and an insignificant amount of scrub pine and fir covering a few elevations, the area is almost totally lacking in natural resources. Its soil composition covers a wide range all the way from a light sandy layer to the heavy gumbo cover that varies from two to six inches in depth over thousands of square miles of arable land.

The best of this soil has been scientifically classified not better than fragile or marginal, placing it in the lower brackets as to fertility. The shame of it all is that knowledge of this condition was not discovered or, worse yet, was withheld from the public for more than ten years after the big westward migration into this area had ended. To add to this, rainfall figures presented in publicity materials disseminated by advertising agencies, chambers of commerce, the railroads, and various government agencies were not only misleading but were actually full of errors. These conditions add substantially to the explanation for the conditions that developed in this area after 1917.

The climax of the whole situation, strangely enough and yet not so strangely, results from the location of Sumatra and its surrounding territory—in the middle of the driest of this arid land, many miles from running streams or natural bodies of water. In addition, its high elevation prohibits irrigation of its thousands of arable acres because of one simple but basic law of physics—water finds it very difficult to run up hill.

Who were the people who worked hard to overcome these adversities and succeeded for a time in making the necessary adjustments for them to live fairly normal and happy lives? They differed little from the other 300,000 individuals who had come to Montana from nearly every state in the Union and many foreign countries. They represented scores of occupations and professions and were motivated by the same pressures, emotions, and interests as most other human beings. Yet they were different—they had to be to pull up stakes from well established and successful businesses, professions, and farms to face the uncertainties and risks in a new country with its great distances and almost total lack of contemporary comforts.

It took an abundance of the pioneer spirit and a lot of intestinal fortitude—plain old guts, if you please. It took faith in the productivity of this new and unbroken land. It took confidence in their own abilities to make the adjustments necessary to cope with the extreme cold of long winters and the intense heat of the summer season. And, being human and for the most part just ordinary people, some had what it took and some did not. But even those who really had it found themselves occasionally helpless in the relentless battle against the uncontrollable elements of time, weather, and nature.

Who were these people? If the telephone had been available to Sumatra people by 1917 the city directory would have contained the following names and pursuits: Ike Bartelson, livery stable and feed barn; George Bartlett, postmaster; Harvey Bartlett, repair shop and garage; Thad Bassett, drayage; Thomas Brown, farm implements; Jack Buchanan, blacksmith; Clint Cady, section worker; Ben Carlen, general store; John Carlson, section foreman; Jim Chittick, elevator manager; N.H. Davis, high school principal; W. E. (Cotton) Duff, saloon; Charley Eaton, livery stable; Henry Enger, general store; David Finch, banker, Bill Gutman, wholesale oil; John Hall, Land Commissioner; Henry Hayden, mechanic; Bruce Hayes, hotel keeper; Jess Hayes, railroad agent; Ben Hayward, well-driller; Minnie Herbold, hotel keeper; Helen Holmes, grade teacher; L. C. Howard, high school teacher; Richard Imhoff, general store; Harry Jaffee, general store; Rufus Jones, carpenter; Frank Kemp, lumber yard; Augie Krause, bartender; Henry Kreider, mail carrier; Mayme Lawson, bank teller; Paul McDonald, banker; Fred Messmer, carpenter; J. E. Midgett, physician and pharmacist; Bill Morris, assistant postmaster; Vic Morris, banker; Wes Mulherin, barber; Flace Phebus, railroad warehouseman; Claude Pickard, railroad agent; Charley Plumb, railroad operator; Henry Polk, newspaper editor; Robert L. Ross, bank manager; Edna Senn, teacher; William Steel, restaurateur; Walter Sweeney, general merchandise; Henry Thayer, lumber and hardware merchant; Fred Wilson, land locator.

If extended to the outlying areas the little town would have been surrounded by a network of lines reaching out 15 to 30 miles in all directions and providing service to more then 150 families who usually regarded Sumatra as their market place. Included in the rural section of the directory would have been the following names: Adams, Agler, Ahern, Atkins, Ayers, Babcock, Bartelson, Behmetiuk, Bender, Bernhard, Berge, Berry (2), Birch, Bliss, Bonser, Booher, Brain, Brashear, Broeder, Brauer, Buchan, Burkhart, Burnett, Burton, Chilcote, Christian, Clark, Cody, Cosgrove, Davis (2), Day, Dirrim, Donahue, Dorothy (2), Dorn, Dorsh, DuBois, Ducummon, Duncan, Dutton, Elliott, Fellers, Finch, Flindt, Flint, Franzel, Galloway, Garnett, Gauman, Gibbs, Glazier, Gordon, Gray, Grebe (3), Green, Gunderson, Guth, Guthridge, Guy, Hall, Hamre (2), Harris, Hauck, Hayes, Hecker, Herbold, Hersitz(2), Hill, Hjelvic (2), Hiller, Hoagland, Hohn, Holmes, Horowitz, Howell, Hudson, Hurd, Isaacs, Jackson, Jennings, Johnson, Johnston, Joines (2), Jones, Kanta, Keckler, Kent (2), Kerner, Kesterson, Kicker, Kincheloe, King (2), Kirkpatrick, Kluk, Klundt, Koch (2), Kuhnes, LaFurge, Lawson, Liffrig, Linde, Lindley, Lindsay, Lyons, Marvin (2), Mathwig, McConnell, McDonald, McGivern (2) , McQuiston, McWilliams, Messer, Messmer, Mockerman, Morris (2), Morton, Neiter, Nelson, Nipp, Noble, Nybrand, O'Conner, O'Dea, Orton, Payton (2), Peacock, Peterson, Potts, Priebe, Randolph, Rasque, Reagor, Reichenbach, Richard, Riddle (3), Rignold, Robertson, Rodewald, Roehl, Rothwell, Roush, Rowland, Rudquist, Ruskosky (2), Russell, Ryan, Sager, Sample, Schleder, Schoessler, Shaeffer, Siemion, Sloan (2), Smith (2), Snyder, Soderquist, Sollie, Stein, Stensvold, Stevens (2), Stilwell, Stockland, Stokke, Tallman, Thomas, Thompson (3), Trapp, Turner, VanBuskirk, Vestal, Wagner, Walker, Wedemeyer, Wedeward, West, Whitney,

Wiecks, Williams, Wilson (2), Witt, Wygle, Yates, York, Youderian, Zager, Zaharko, Zawada, Zimmerman.

Chapter VII

1917 was an important year for us and our town, as it most certainly was for much of the rest of the planet. For nearly two years and a half the greatest struggle between nations in the world's history had been in progress. Although not actively engaged in the hostilities, all parts of the U.S. had been greatly affected by the war, including the sparsely settled state of Montana and even the little towns like Sumatra. With shortages of many materials essential to military action, demand grew for increased production of metals and lumber as well as many of the foodstuffs and meat products from Montana's farms. Employment was high throughout the state and personal income set an all-time record up to 1918.

With the declaration of war by this country on April 6, 1917, demand for materials produced by Montana's farms and industries continued to grow and market prices maintained the gradual rise evident during the previous three years. Despite strikes in the mines at Butte, the state as a whole was probably in the best financial condition of its entire history. A spirit of optimism reigned. This mood seeped down to even the smallest communities such as Sumatra.

Following the winter of 1916-1917 spring conditions favorable to another good crop persisted in Rosebud County and contiguous areas. Dad was looking forward to another good harvest and the Midgetts would be able to pay off a large part of the debt we had accumulated from building the house on the farm and setting up the drug store. In May he hired Hubert Morris to haul the 500 bushels of stored wheat to the elevator. At a price of $2.60 per bushel he realized enough to pay up the balance of his account with the Minneapolis Drug Company for the original order of goods for the store. A substantial payment was also made to the local bank whose manager, Bob Ross, had loaned Dad the money to buy and remodel the store building. For the next seven or eight years Bob was to be our greatest friend and benefactor, and when things really got tough he was always there to help. After renting the house in Hibbard for a year Dad sold it in late 1916 on a monthly payment plan and applied the money on the installments to the Federal Land Bank that had financed the ranch buildings with the farm as collateral.

Decisions, decisions, decisions! This was the time for probably the most important options Dad ever had to consider up to that time. The death of Uncle Ross turned out to be a much more serious blow than we had thought. Everything done in late 1916 had been predicated on the expectation of his recovery and his ability to manage the store for the next two or three years at least. This was all changed when his health deteriorated rapidly during the winter and by the first of March 1917, Dad knew he would have to make some changes in his plans.

Much of the decision-making hinged on the question of what was to be done with the store, for state laws prohibited the operation of a drug store without the services of a registered pharmacist. Although the store had done fairly well during the few months of its existence and would probably do better when the weather warmed up, it was doubtful that it could support a full-time pharmacist in addition to paying for itself. There seemed to be only one solution to the problem—Dad would have to qualify as a registered pharmacist. Since this would require a great amount of time in study and preparation for the state examinations, more than he could possibly find in his present situation, other arrangements had to be made. During the summer of 1917 I spent most of my time at the store while Dad took care of the work on the farm. Elizabeth was thirteen now and able to help me one or two days a week. Between us we held down the fort.

A second important consideration was where it would be best for us to live—to continue on the farm or move into town. After moving twice in the past two and one-half years, Mother would have been well satisfied to stay where we were. But, as always, when such choices were necessary she did not allow her personal feelings to unduly affect the final decision. In this case they agreed that a home in town was the next order of business.

By the fall of 1918 all four of us kids would be in school with Olive just starting the first grade. Travel back and forth to town five days a week would require the use of the Model T or a two-mile walk to school which was a little too much for a six-year-old. Either Dad would have to take us in and then return home if the farm work required his efforts or I would drive the car to school, leaving him without transportation in case of a sick call. Since there would be no one else to keep the store open, Dad would have to spend the mornings at the ranch and keep the store open in the afternoons.

While this projected arrangement seemed to be adequate as long as the weather was warm, it was clear that it would not work in the winter time. By the first of August 1917, another decision was made—a move into town as soon as a suitable place to live could be found and Dad could locate someone to look after the farm, at least for the winter. I believe Dad was still not certain he wanted to leave the ranch and may have considered the idea of selling the store and moving back to the ranch in the spring. Late in the fall we moved into a four-room tar papered shack on the southwest edge of Sumatra. An ad was placed in two or three of the state's daily papers offering the store for sale or lease but no serious offers were received.

Dad's hopes and prospects for definite improvement of his financial situation received a serious setback when, late in the afternoon of the tenth of August, he saw what promised to be a 30 bushel per acre crop knocked down by a hail storm lasting about fifteen minutes. He watched the approaching clouds from the front porch of the store and, although the storm was much less powerful in town, he sensed its severity at the ranch and drove home immediately. I shall never forget the scene. He walked into the field west of the house and realized the extent of damage to the crop which that morning had been his pride and joy. When he returned he sat on a box and buried his head in his hands. It was one of the few times I ever saw him cry.

The leavings threshed out less than ten bushels per acre and his net income from its sale came to less than $2,000 instead of the four or five thousand he had anticipated. Most of the late vegetable crop was also lost in the storm so Mother was unable to put up our usual supply of canned goods. This of course added an expense we had not anticipated and most of our vegetable foods came out of store-bought cans that winter and the spring of 1918.

Although none of us anticipated it at the time, I now realize that 1917 was the beginning of the end as far as Sumatra and that part of Montana was concerned. Everything still looked good in the southeastern part of the state but the drought had already struck in most of the northern and central counties east of the Rockies. Extremely hot, dry stretches of weather in July had seared the green fields of June and produced the dust storms of August and September. Wheat production in the "Golden Triangle" north of Great Falls and in the Judith Basin, two of the highest yielding areas in Montana, had dropped by at least half in comparison with the previous five-year average yield. This was but a harbinger of what was to come during the next few years in our area. What would have happened to us and many of our friends and neighbors if we could have foreseen the next five years? I guess it will always be only an interesting conjecture, but I am inclined to think things might have been much different for a lot of people.

*   *   *   *

Soon after war was declared in April 1917, a congressional measure was passed that had a profound effect upon the whole state of Montana and especially our sparsely populated portion of it. The Selective Service Act became effective in August and in the first lottery drawing that covered all males between the ages 21 to 30 three of the young men were taken from our community. This was a serious blow since a large percentage of our meager populace was made up of young single men and newly married couples who had come to Montana with hopes of getting their share of this big, fresh, young country. Each monthly drawing over the next year dug into the remaining supply of young men, and many of their young wives also left the state.

By November, the first of the draftees had completed basic training at Fort Lewis, Washington, and were on their way to the east coast embarkation ports. When the first troop train went through on the Milwaukee Road, we kids were let out of school to watch it.

Everybody waved little American flags and the depot was decorated with flags and red, white, and blue bunting. During the next twelve months this scene was repeated many times and when the trains stopped, which was not often, the doughboys were showered with candy, cookies, and small favors. Some of the boys who left from the Sumatra area were Burr Berry, John Schoessler, Harold Glazier, Earl Babcock, Floyd Williams, Harry Koch, Art Hecker, Oscar Peterson, Art Peterson, Harley Burling, Augie Krause, Henry Juth, Matt Hjelvik, Charley Randolph, George Bender, Jr., Joe Cosgrove, Dave and Dan Finch, Clen and Gail Kent, Joe and Moody Rasque, Toady Raygor, Howard Payton, Karl Wedeward, one of the Zaharko boys, Vic and Bill Morris, Francis Riddle, and one of the Grebe boys. Most of them had waited for their draft notices but a few, including Vic and Bill Morris, had gone to Forsyth and volunteered. Both of them were quite short, Vic about an inch taller than his brother. When they took their physicals Bill was rejected when he failed to make the minimum height, but a few weeks later the height requirement was reduced and Bill was accepted on his second enlistment try late in 1917.

In late summer of 1917 the country as a whole was rampant with patriotic fervor and almost everyone volunteered to do what he could for the war effort. The farmers were urged by the War Department to plant as many acres as possible into grain production to furnish food for our Allies in Europe whose lands had been ravaged by more than three years of warfare. With so many young men in the service, help was short and every farmer extended himself to the limit to plant as much acreage as possible that fall. A shortage of seed wheat that had become very serious in the northern counties was not yet critical in Rosebud County so "full production" was the motto of wheat growers in the Sumatra area.

In their endeavor to aid the "common cause" my folks fell in line as far as crop production was concerned. Although he had decided to leave the farm, Dad applied to the Federal Farm Loan Association for money to buy seed for more than 100 acres he had under cultivation. With the help of a couple of our farmer neighbors it was all planted by the middle of October and we could only hope for at least one more good crop year to partially repay the added financial burden contracted by the addition of another five hundred dollars to the mortgage on the ranch.

For the first two months of the 1917-18 school year we continued to travel back and forth to town. I think we all hated to think of leaving the ranch as the two years we had lived there had been very happy and healthy ones. Mother had been very busy raising a family of four with all the extra work peculiar to life on a farm. Although Elizabeth and I helped a great deal by taking care of the stock and doing many of the odd jobs around the place we did not make up for the time, effort and mature judgment she had lost due to Dad's absence at the store or on sick calls.

Despite the hard work and the sixteen-hour days the year round she was still very patient with us kids. I can't remember that either she or Dad ever complained about their lot in life—at least not in our presence. It certainly is not my intention here to paint my parents as saints or even religious fanatics but I am sure they always believed that their faith in God and practice of the Golden Rule, together with their own diligence, were enough to carry them through any situation they might encounter, no matter how difficult.

*   *   *   *

Perhaps one reason why the folks were not eager to leave the ranch was the natural beauty of its location. I never appreciated or even realized this until my visits back to the area during the past few years. The common impression of eastern Montana is of a great expanse of wasteland consisting of barren rolling hills dotted with sage brush, cactus and grease wood, almost completely barren of trees and green grass. This, I agree, is and probably was typical of much of this area, but the location of our house and the panorama viewed from it in all directions leaves anything but an unfavorable impression on the beholder.

The house, facing south toward the road, was located about fifty yards north of the south line of our section and about a hundred yards east of its north-south center line. The flat area surrounding it was about two hundred yards square and was the highest part of the entire section so we could see long distances in all directions except straight west. The barn was located about two hundred feet east of the house on the brow of a hill sloping over a quarter of a mile down to the stock pond. Since it was about twelve feet high it cut off the view directly east from the house but otherwise we could see for miles and miles. To the northeast a succession of low hills gradually led up to the divide between Muggins Creek, which runs along the east edge of Sumatra, and Blacktail Creek, which rises about seven or eight miles northeast. To the southeast we could see for a distance of eight or ten miles down the course of Muggins Creek as it flows south toward the Yellowstone River, over thirty miles away. Our vista to the south and southwest was practically unbroken for a distance of four or five miles and we could see smoke rising from chimneys of a half dozen homesteads including the Adams, Burnetts, Schleders, Ross Dorothys, and Ernest Stevens.

Although the view directly west was closer than the others it was the most interesting of all. After leaving our west line the road climbed a hill two or three hundred feet high topped by a sandstone ridge and scattered scrub pines. It was beautiful in the early summer when the hillsides were covered with green grass and an abundance of the most gorgeous multi-colored native flowers I have ever seen. Around the north end of the hills one could glimpse the Big Snowy Mountains southeast of Lewistown on a clear day—a distance of almost eighty miles. Frequently on a hot summer day we could see a mirage of trees along the Musselshell River, about twelve miles away and many feet below our normal range of vision. A view of ten miles or more of rolling hills covered by sage brush was visible to the north and probably we could have seen the derricks of the oil wells of the West Sumatra Oil Field on Rattlesnake Creek if they had existed then.

The winter scene was equally beautiful. With anywhere from a few inches to two feet of snow on the ground from late November to early March, the bright sun produced a panorama of solid white extending for miles in all directions broken only by the few scrubby trees off to the south and west and the smoke from a dozen chimneys of the surrounding farm homes. The overwhelming quiet of the night was broken by the cry of a coyote searching for a nice fat sage hen nesting under a leafy bush covered by a mantle of snow or by the hoot of a little snow owl hunting a field mouse out looking for a few stray grains of wheat—such were the eerie sounds of the winter stillness. We loved it all and hated to give it up.

Viewing it in retrospect I understand why the folks did not decide to build in Sumatra until winter was half over. By then the store had been operating a full year, business was gradually picking up, and Dad's medical practice was sufficient to produce enough income to convince him he could make a good living by working at it full time. More and more people had settled in the area and there was little indication it would change in the foreseeable future.

Rufus and Earl Jones were again hired in February 1918 to plan and construct our new home in Sumatra. It was to be large enough to serve as a combination residence and hospital providing Dad's seriously ill patients with a place to stay while being treated. Of the six large bedrooms, two upstairs and the front one downstairs were kept available for seriously ill or injured people brought in from the countryside. This served a double purpose. It saved all except his most critical patients from heavy hospital expenses and it eliminated long difficult trips over rough and muddy roads to the patients' rural homes. By July 1, 1918, the new home was ready to move into and we were all glad to get out of the tarpaper shack ahead of the hot weather of another typical Montana summer. Meanwhile, Dad had found a renter for the ranch and had sold all the machinery and livestock, except Cricket and Daisy, to the new occupant. Now that Dad had made another decision, it was quite final that we were not going back to the ranch—not at least for a few years.

Through 1916 and 1917 people of the area had been quite prosperous with their good crops bringing high prices. Much of the business in the drug store was on a cash basis and for the most part Dad had been paid for his services to the sick. Everything looked good and we had no reason to believe it would change soon or to regret having come to Montana.

*   *   *   *

After hostilities were declared in April of 1917 the government discovered that it took money to wage a war and by June, the first of a series of Liberty Loan drives was sponsored by the Treasury Department. The first campaign kicked off on June 5 to raise a sum of over twelve billion dollars. Institutions of all kinds including civic and service clubs, churches, banks, commercial and benevolent organizations, and even schools were enlisted to use all their facilities to aid in the common effort. Children were asked to save their nickels and pennies and one period a week was set aside in the schools to collect the money that was used to buy War Savings Stamps that were pasted in booklets. When sufficient quantities of these had accumulated they were converted into Liberty Bonds in denominations of $25 or $50. The bonds actually cost the purchaser $18.75 or $37.50 and were set up to mature at the end of ten years.

Many local speakers were recruited to appear before every community gathering. After moving into town both Dad and Mother volunteered their talents and spare time to the cause as the most effective way of showing their patriotism and love for their country. Although I never heard her talk I learned Mother was regarded as a very effective speaker and both she and Dad received the highest citizen awards given by the government when the war was over. In four separate drives over a period of seventeen months more than twenty-two billion dollars were raised in the forty-eight states for the conduct of the war. Montana was near the top in per capita sales of Liberty and Victory bonds in 1917 and 1918.

By March 21, 1918 more than 300,000 American troops had arrived on the French battlefront. Although we didn't realize it at the time, their accelerated appearance in various sectors signaled the beginning of the end of the war. Combat mortality was high during the next eight months and it wasn't long before the names of Montana boys showed up in the daily casualty lists in the newspapers. By the end of the struggle, out of a total of approximately 350,000 dead and wounded U.S. troops almost 3500 were Montana boys. Although the state ranked in the lowest ten percent in U.S. population statistics, the number of war casualties from Montana placed her 27th out of 48 and above Washington, Nebraska and Oregon with three to five times as much population. A review of figures years later revealed that an error in determining its draft quota in 1917 and 1918 resulted in Rosebud County and the state of Montana furnishing considerably greater manpower than their proportionate shares. It follows that the Sumatra area also supplied a larger number of young men than its rightful quota but little complaint was ever heard.

I mentioned that the feeling of patriotism and loyalty to country was very strong at this time. At times this feeling developed into an emotion bordering on hysteria and fanaticism. We saw overt evidence of this feeling when a few families of German origin and even some whose only sin was having come from central Europe were suspected of being pro-German sympathizers and even spying for the governments of their fatherlands. Since there were quite a few settlers of German origin with such names as Mathwig, Hecker, Kicker, Kreider, Wedeward and even Zaharko, Zawada, Kluk, and Behmetiuk, they were suspect.

Rumors of threats were frequent and a few books were burned but clearer heads prevailed in our part of the country. I don't recall anyone being driven from the region or landing in jail as a traitor to his country. In fact, quite a few volunteers into military service came from these very loyal citizens and their financial contributions to the cause either equaled or surpassed those of many of their neighbors.

*　　　　*　　　　*　　　　*

The school year of 1917-18 had gotten off to a good start on the 16th of September with only three of us in the sophomore year of high school—Gladys Williams and Elizabeth Schleder, who had attended the Catholic Academy in Miles City, and me. The size of the grade school continued to increase with the enrollment of ten new first graders but the only two graduating eighth graders the previous May had moved away from the area. The freshman class that fall was limited to one girl, Bernice Turner, who finished the eighth grade at the McTwiggan School, about twenty miles north of Sumatra. Mr. and Mrs. Davis continued to teach the high school subjects with the help of Miss Bess Bedell, who had come from Chicago. She taught the English and Latin classes. Only one second floor room was completed that fall so all classes were held there and Principal Davis had full use of his office.

With enrollment still so small, the school had not yet become the social center of the community. However, many meetings were held in the downstairs rooms and all Protestant church services were held in the first floor east room. With the conversion of the old town hall into a drug store, public dances and other programs and parties were also held in the new building until, in the fall of 1918, Tom Brown built his implement shed with an upstairs meeting hall.

After moving into our new home we soon discovered all of our problems had not yet been solved. The lots Dad had purchased from the Sumatra Townsite Company were located on a ridge on the east edge of town. They were about fifty feet or more above the flat where most of the village had developed. From our home we looked down on most of the town and our view of the surrounding area was quite open in most directions, but not as pleasant to the eye as that from the ranch. We could easily see the ranch buildings with the background of the sand hills and scrub pines in the west.

Dad had planned to have a water well dug near the house hoping we were close enough to Muggins Creek to strike a water table at a relatively shallow level. However, all tests made in the immediate area showed very little water and most of that contained too much alkali for human consumption. This meant the only source of our drinking and cooking supply would continue to be the railroad tank cars on which we had largely relied for the past three years. At least twice a week we hauled the water from the tank in two ten gallon milk cans in the back seat of the Model T, contributing to the wear and tear on the car and its final early demise. This supply of water was supplemented by rain water off the roof caught in a barrel located at the southwest corner of the house just outside the kitchen door. During most of the winter the water supply came from melted snow that was usually quite plentiful from the first of December to the middle of March. Livestock owned by the townspeople got most of their water from the East and West lakes formed by the railroad embankments on both sides of town. During colder weather it was necessary to cut holes in the ice before the animals could drink and the owners took turns performing this task.

The care and treatment of Dad's patients was made much easier by the accommodations provided by the big house. Even though he set regular office hours and requested that patients be brought into town when possible, more and more of his time was taken by increasing number of calls requiring travel to the rural areas. How to keep the store open with Elizabeth and me in school was a serious problem. Mother could help out frequently for a few hours at a time but she had her own work to do and she always regarded the care of her own family as her greatest responsibility. This resulted in the store being closed many hours each week when Dad was called out of town until we worked out an agreement with Principal Davis to let me out of school when I was through with my classes. We also developed a plan of accepting orders by mail or leaving them through a slot in the front door when there was no one there. If we had what they wanted we would mail it out C.O.D., or if we didn't have it we would order it for them. This saved our customers the necessity of a long trip to Forsyth or Melstone to buy their drugs.

During this time the problem of what to do about a pharmacist still weighed on Dad's mind. He had written the State Board of Pharmacy in May 1917 explaining his situation and seeking their advice. Being a registered physician was, of course, all in his favor and after investigating the circumstances, the board granted Dad a two-year moratorium with the stipulation that he not fill the prescriptions of other doctors. At the end of that time he either would have to have a registered pharmacist or pass the pharmacy exams himself.

The restriction regarding filling prescriptions had very little effect on his business since, with the exception of Dr. Krause who came to Melstone in 1918, there were no other practicing physicians for fifty miles around. Dad, himself, had never been a prescription type doctor but instead doled out his pills or a bottle of medicine directly from a couple of cases he carried with him everywhere he went. This was the way he was trained to practice medicine and it wasn't until many years later when the pharmaceutical companies had concocted too many remedies to carry in a couple of small cases that he started writing prescriptions to be filled at the new-fashioned pharmacies with their hundreds and hundreds of pills, powders, salves and liquids.

Still doubting that the business in Sumatra and surrounding area would ever amount to enough to support the hiring of a pharmacist, Dad chose his second option and in his spare time began to study textbooks on pharmacy supplemented by the U.S. Pharmacopoeia and catalogues from a number of the drug manufacturers in the country. In September 1919 he went to Helena and took the examination but came home very discouraged, knowing he had failed to pass it. Time for another try was extended six months and during the next few months he spent considerable time studying some of the tests that had been given previously. In March 1920 he made the trip back to Helena and tried again. This time he was successful and received his license to practice pharmacy in Montana on April 16 signed by F.J. Adams, president of the Pharmacy Board. Although he had no occasion to apply his capabilities as a druggist until many years after he left Sumatra, he kept his license effective by paying the state renewal each year.

The growing season of 1918 began with a critical lack of soil moisture as snowfall during the winter had been considerably less than in recent years. However, the green shoots of wheat planted the previous fall looked good until the middle of April when the rains that usually fell during the next month or two failed to arrive. By the middle of June farmers of the area had generally concluded that the drought had reached Rosebud County and there was very little that could be done about it. One year of it wouldn't be so bad following the four or five good crops and high prices they had received every season since 1913. I doubt many of the settlers who took their farming seriously ever entertained the idea that dry conditions would or could continue long enough to hurt them seriously. Yields of five to ten bushels were the common run that year and in many cases it hardly paid to harvest the crop. But hope springs eternal and most of the growers bought seed wheat with borrowed money and sowed most of their cultivated acreage again in the fall. The high prices of farm products persisted and were a very strong factor in influencing the decision of the wheat farmers to try it again.

Another important effect of the dry hot summer was a great shrinkage of the wild hay crop on which most ranchers depended to provide winter feed for their horses and cattle. Although few farmers had gone into extensive stock production it was still necessary to harvest a good supply of the native grasses to supplement their cultivated crops because of the long cold winters in eastern Montana. By the middle of January 1919, most of the haystacks around the country had almost disappeared and feed was being shipped in from other areas, particularly South Dakota and Minnesota. Prices were high and were greatly increased by high freight rates into Montana. Many farmers were paying $70 or more per ton that, combined with cost of freight and transportation from rail to ranch, brought total cost to approximately $100.

Some relief came too late when Governor Stewart put pressure on the Interstate Commerce Commission to reduce freight rates on all stock food brought into Montana. Even with the high prices paid for the feed most of the farmers would have made it through the long cold winter of 1918-19 if the imported hay had been of good quality. However, it was soon discovered that it had very little nourishment and animals to whom it was fed lost weight and became weaker and weaker as the winter lingered on. An investigation at the points of production revealed that most of the imported hay was cut from dry lake beds and was ordinarily not even harvested in those areas. Needless to say, hundreds of cattle died before the spring thaws set in and quite a few of their owners offered their places for sale in the spring of 1919.

Since farm land in this part of Montana had not been under cultivation nearly as long as that in other areas of the state invasions of grasshoppers and cutworms had not yet struck the area in the destructive numbers reported from other sections. However, predictions were made by the State Extension Service that all of Rosebud County and other surrounding areas could expect an invasion of the insects by the summer of 1919. Preparations to meet the pests were started during the previous winter when the County Agent at Forsyth spent many weeks mixing a compound of bran mash and insect killing poisons that was distributed to the farmers on the basis of need and acreage planted. Mechanical spreaders had not yet been invented so most of it was scattered by hand over the fields from horse drawn conveyances when the insects made their appearance in June and July. The treatment was quite expensive and required much larger amounts than could be provided, so on many farms it was not very effective and the pests created a great deal of damage to grain fields already devastated by dry weather. However, the infestation in the western part of the county was not as heavy as in the drainage areas of both the Yellowstone and Missouri rivers. Garden crops, although somewhat short due to the lack of rainfall in June, were not greatly affected by the hoppers and Mother put up her usual winter supply of canned vegetables.

Chapter VIII

By the end of the school year in May 1918 we felt we were really a part of the community and were making some contributions to its development in a number of ways. Our active interest in the Protestant church and its organizations did much to create great amount of concern for the institution and helped it over some difficult times during the next few years. Dad had shown his intense interest in the schools and education in general by working hard for passage of the bond issue for the new building in the spring of 1916 and a year later was a successful candidate for the local school board. For the next several years he continued in that capacity with the other two members, Wright Dorothy, representing the south end of the district, and D. Van Rowland, who lived in the Blacktail country northeast of town. The clerk of the board was George Bartlett, who had been appointed Postmaster in 1916. George was deformed from a back injury in his youth, but his ailment did not interfere with his intellectual ability or to any serious extent with his physical efficiency as a mechanic.

Despite a lack of much spare time Dad never sidestepped an obligation to serve his community and help it develop into a viable society that could contribute to the best interests of its residents and those in its trade area. He was also a member of the local board of directors of the Federal Farm Loan Association which passed on loans made to the farmers and ranchers of the region. All of these activities took hours of time already filled to the limit with the seemingly endless and exhausting duties connected with alleviating the miseries of the sick and injured of the community, keeping the drug store open most of the time, and trying his best to make the farm a paying proposition. Any one of these would have been enough for the average person. All of this plus raising a family of four lively children and providing them with the opportunity and encouragement to make the most of their talents and capabilities.

I have wondered many times where all the physical, mental, and moral strength required for such a full and exhausting life came from. After mentally reviewing that ten year period, 1914-24, and all the trials and tribulations our family faced and overcame, I come closer to understanding how they were able to hang on and maintain their faith in the Sumatra area long after many of their friends and neighbors had pulled stakes and left the country. To maintain their sanity and poise under such circumstances required more than normal human strength and perseverance.

My meditations have led me to five elementary principles that made all of this possible. Without attempting to put them in order I have decided those five postulates are: (1) the closely knit family that, through their willingness to help each other under all circumstances, made it possible to accomplish much more than the six of us could have done as individuals; (2) Dad's dedication to his profession and the Hippocratic Oath through which he had pledged to minister to all who needed his services to the best of his ability at all times and under all conditions. He carried this precept over into all of his relationships—business, social, and religious. I am certain this practice resulted in much satisfaction in many situations that might otherwise have been discouraging to say the least; (3) a helpmate who was always optimistic about the future even when things looked their darkest and thus helped him through many very trying circumstances; (4) his belief in the goodness of all with whom he came in contact and conviction that if he treated them with respect they would respond in kind. In all my association with Dad I never heard him utter a disparaging word about a fellow man; (5) his complete belief and faith in a supreme being as a source of help in time of need and his sense of appreciation to God as shown by his unwavering dedication to the practice of his religion and his attitude toward other people.

It is not my intention to portray our family as totally without fault or devoid of human error. I am sure they made many mistakes but, due to their attitude toward life, were less affected by their adversities than persons who do not have such a philosophy to support them. Many were the mornings when the folks woke up to the pressures of overwhelming problems that would have crushed the average family. Other than a lack of time to do everything that required their attention, probably their greatest problem was ready cash to buy necessities or pay obligations when due. I recall many times, especially from 1919 on, when Dad wondered where their next expendable dollar was coming from. At times even a few cents for us kids to put in the collection plate were hard to come by, and Mom would take a few dozen eggs to the store on Saturday and bring home fifty or sixty cents or buy two or three grocery items she needed.

Dad kept his credit at the bank good but he did not use it any oftener than necessary. Receipts from sales of drug merchandise from the store were all deposited in a special account and were used to pay for replacement of merchandise and to make payments on the building itself. Dad depended principally on his medical practice to produce the funds necessary to support the family. In good crop years these were supplemented by any net profit after making the annual payments on the farm and the new home in town.

This rather complex arrangement of his finances seemed to work out well through the good crop years when not only Dad but most of the other settlers were making money and had proved up on their homesteads. But in 1918 hot dry summer winds shriveled the wheat kernels in the milk and blew clouds of dust for miles and miles over the dry land country. Combined with the drop in market prices of wheat and other grains following the end of the war everybody was financially affected although not seriously enough to become discouraged or lose their faith in Montana and their optimism for the future. However, Dad's situation was considerably different from most of his neighbors because he was engaged in three enterprises rather than only one as was the usual case. With everyone finding themselves with less money to spend but still needing medical services and drug store products Dad found he was making more calls and charging them or taking farm products such as two or three chickens, a sack of potatoes, or half a hog in payment for services rendered. In the store we were forced to open credit accounts but became more and more cautious as to whom we granted the courtesy. As the years passed and crop growing conditions failed to improve, this situation gradually worsened.

*   *   *   *

Meanwhile U.S. war operations in Europe had expanded and increasing numbers of American doughboys were engaged in the struggle. By July 1918, conscription had produced approximately two million men for the armed services. This number was supplemented greatly by voluntary enlistments. It all became quite personal when in August, Tony Schleder, a friend of mine, and I went to Forsyth and tried to enlist but were turned down. He was 17 years old and I had just turned 16 in July.

The armies of the Entente Powers were gradually retreating toward their homeland but not without heavier casualties on both sides. The lists in the newspaper grew longer and more boys from Rosebud County were included in them. By August reports were widespread that scattered German forces were surrendering in large groups. Predictions were being made by U.S. government officials that it would only be a matter of months before the war would all be over. It still came as a surprise to most of the nation when early in November reports circulated that some high German officials had deserted the Kaiser and it was now a matter of days before an armistice would be signed.

When the announcement was made in the newspapers on November 10 that the German armies had capitulated and articles of surrender were to be signed the next day there was much rejoicing. I'll never forget the early morning of the 11th when news of the armistice came over the wire. I was awakened by the explosion of a powerful torpedo set off down by the railroad tracks followed a few minutes later by shotgun blasts and firecrackers all over town. People ran up and down Main Street shouting and crying with the overwhelming joy of realization that the long, tragic struggle was over. The climax of the event as far as we were concerned occurred when Dad in his unbounded enthusiasm, took his 12 gauge shotgun and blasted a hole through the upper part of the store's facade. To my knowledge the hole was never repaired and became a haven for the birds in later years.

The great happiness produced by the termination of hostilities was tempered a few months later when the Spanish influenza struck the U.S. in epidemic proportions. It seemed to originate among the servicemen in the east coast camps, probably brought back by the boys returning from Europe. The disease spread rapidly across the country and soon reports of heavy mortality were coming out of the larger cities. Large numbers of cases in the west coast encampments were fatal and by the first of the year in 1919 almost every passenger train traveling east was carrying at least one extra baggage coach full of pine boxes wrapped in U.S. flags.

Although rural areas with their scattered populations were hit less hard than the more populous regions, nearly every family was touched by the disease during the next three or four months. My sister, Olive, and I were the first in our family to take to our beds and become two of Dad's early flu victims. The other beds in our home were soon filled with sick people brought in from outlying areas. For what seemed like an endless number of weeks those rooms and many others that had been offered throughout the town were occupied. Well people proffered their services to care for the less fortunate and Dad, through the weekly paper, was urging ill people in the rural area to bring any sick members of their families into town for treatment if possible. Since by 1919 most of the settlers had automobiles and many of the principal roads had been graded and some graveled, transportation was not the problem it had been five years earlier.

All this cooperation and teamwork by the people of the area made it possible for Dad to treat many more patients than he conceivably could have done if he had had to do a great deal of traveling. As it was he was going night and day and during the height of the siege he was seeing fifteen to twenty sick people a day. How he kept his strength for such a long period of time has always been a mystery to me. I am sure he could have done it only with help from a power greater than himself.

For more than a month through January and February all of our extra beds were full of sick people including Mother who suffered as much from being unable to take care of her family and help Dad as she did from the illness itself. At the end of the long spell of illness a review of his account books showed he had treated approximately 400 patients over a three-month period with a loss of only two flu sufferers. Both of these had developed complications and were in advanced stages of pneumonia before he had been called. He had rushed them to the Roundup hospital where they died within a few days.

This ministration to the afflicted involved their consuming thousands of doses of three of the oldest and most dependable of the myriad remedies prescribed by the medical profession. Dad relied on aspirin for the relief of the aches and pains, quinine to reduce fever, and a big dose of castor oil or Epsom salts to clean out the digestive system. These three drugs plus the application of cold packs and mustard plasters and plenty of bedrest made up his complete formula for treatment. No antibiotics, sulfanilamides, multi-vitamins, or other effective remedies produced by modern science. To my mind this fact makes his achievement in this test of his medical competency all the greater. But then, as was true during his entire career in the medical profession, he took no credit for the ultimate cure of the sick. He was only the dispenser of the healing agent and his principal function was knowing what, when, and how to administer the most effective remedy in each case.

In addition to his good fortune in saving the lives of so many people through his services, Dad enjoyed a welcome bonus in the considerable improvement in his financial condition. At rates of $2.00 for office and $3.00 for house calls plus mileage at five cents per mile on out of town calls most of his patients were able to pay their bills. During the ensuing year his collections were very good and we enjoyed a brief period of limited prosperity.

*   *   *   *

Even though the thoughts and actions of most people during 1918-19 were greatly influenced by the war and the pestilence they had gone through, normal daily tasks and plans still occupied most of their attention. Harvesting the summer's diminished crops and planting the next were still the most important activities in their fall schedules. To make up for their loss of farm income in 1918 a number of farmers of the area found employment in other occupations during the winter. Most of them went to Butte, Roundup, and Klein to work in the mines, while others were employed by the highway department repairing and improving roads in the county after the legislature had appropriated extra state funds for the work.

Another source of income that had developed into an important industry in eastern Montana was sheep raising. After 1908, when millions of acres were opened up for settlement, most of the large cattle ranches gradually disappeared with the influx of homesteaders and the barbed wire strung around their places. In their stead came the sheepmen with their herds numbering in the hundreds of thousands roaming over the arid plains of Rosebud County. By 1914 there were close to six million sheep in the state of Montana, nearly one-sixth of them running the range between the Yellowstone and Missouri Rivers and east of the Musselshell.

Of the eight or ten big sheepmen in the western part of the county only three names remain in my memory. Ted Waddington was probably the kingpin of the industry in the area, running sheep all the way from Miles City to the Musselshell and north of the Milwaukee railroad. Pete Stokke and Svarre Mysee ran their herds mostly south of the railroad in the big expanse of land north of the Yellowstone. The focal point where the herders aimed their flocks at shearing time, late May or early June, was Ingomar, twelve miles east of Sumatra. The shearing plant and warehouse located there was one of the largest in the west and for many years more raw wool was shipped east to the mills than from any other plant in the nation.

By 1918 the increase in the number of flocks in the area had outgrown the capacity of the Ingomar plant. A shortage of water there induced sheepmen to expand their facilities by building a six-shearer facility near the reservoir west of Sumatra. Construction of the new sheds began in the fall with employment for four or five local residents, and the new plant was ready for service for the 1919 shearing season. Most of the shearers were itinerant, following the season northward from the southwestern states, but other jobs such as penning sheep, sacking wool, hauling and loading it into railroad cars were done by workers in the local neighborhood. Although the amount of additional income was not great, it all helped its recipients appreciably and in turn, the entire community profited from the new project.

*   *   *   *

The school year of 1918-19 began with an enrollment increase of both grade and high school pupils. The three of us, Gladys, Elizabeth, and I, still made up the new junior class. Bernice Turner continued to be the only sophomore, but the total registration more than doubled when three eighth grade graduates of the Sumatra school and six others from the rural areas enrolled for their freshman year. With the addition of my sister, Elizabeth, Lois Booher, Letha Hudson, Mamie Morton, Myrtle Smith, and Anna Whitney, the total number of girls was nine. The male contingent stood at five when Ralph Jones, Bill Dirrim, and Bill and Tony Schleder joined me.

Perhaps the main extracurricular activity in the high schools of those days was basketball and most of the schools, considerably larger than Sumatra, were playing inter-school schedules of ten or twelve games. Naturally, we wanted to get into the program too but Principal Davis and the school board decided there weren't enough boys to develop a very competitive aggregation. Since both boys' and girls' teams were included in the state program, the girls also had to wait another year even though their numbers were sufficient to make up a representative team.

We saw to it, however, that we didn't entirely lose that year when, after a great deal of our pestering, the board made arrangements for us to practice in the Jaffe warehouse adjacent to the store. It was 35 or 40 feet long, had only about a twelve foot ceiling and three supports located down the center of the floor. Since there was no stove or heating device it was a little difficult to practice when the thermometer dropped down to zero or below and we had to bundle up and wear heavy mittens to keep warm. Still, we learned a little bit about such fundamental parts of the game as passing, dribbling, and shooting baskets.

I was the only one who had had any experience with a basketball—my freshman year at Forsyth—and Principal Davis had no training along that line, so we just had to do what came naturally. A few of the townsmen, including Dad, Bill and Vic Morris, and Henry Thayer, spent some time with us but I am afraid that, with all their help, we weren't quite ready for competition. By hindsight it is not difficult to understand why the school board, in its wisdom, ruled out our request to play basketball that year.

*   *   *   *

By 1918 problems resulting from the rustic methods of transportation used by settlers in rural areas were gradually being alleviated. A relatively small number were still traveling by horseback or buckboard, but Model Ts or something similar were rapidly making their appearance in most farm yards, and buggy sheds were being converted into garages. The Bartlett shop, originally set up to shoe horses and repair farm machinery, gradually changed into a facility specializing in treating the many ailments to which cars of that early period were prone. Following the death of her husband at Mayo hospital in 1919, Cora Bartlett took on the local agency for Ford cars, which sold for 700 to 800 dollars.

The rows of saddle horses, buckboards, and wagons that lined the hitching rails up and down Main Street had largely disappeared. Although a few farmers and ranchers still depended on their reliable steeds, especially when roads were muddy or snow was deep, the space in front of the stores was now occupied by a Ford, an Overland, a Chevrolet, or, in a few cases, an air-cooled Franklin. Motor trucks were also becoming common and the great distances over which farm products had to be hauled to market shrank rapidly. Trips that had formerly taken at least two days could now be made in a matter of a few hours and it was no trick to drive the 50 miles to the larger marketing centers of Forsyth or Roundup in part of a day.

The world, and especially our part of it, was gradually growing smaller. Besides the development of improved vehicles the most important additional factor was the improvement of roads, both locally and statewide. Planned construction by scientific methods was gradually replacing the old hit-or-miss attempts to provide a passable thoroughfare. Roads were turning into highways twenty to thirty feet in width with gravel surfacing, elevated grades, and good culverts and bridges that wouldn't wash out with every heavy rainstorm or spring runoff. The fear of getting stuck in six inches of mud and gumbo or being stalled by a sudden inundation was pretty well eliminated and travel, both local and to distant points, was much more enjoyable. An important consequence of these improvements was a marked increase in socializing. Where previously about the only communal gathering of the people was an occasional dance in the neighborhood school house and church services on Sunday, the motor car and improvement of roads resulted in numerous public activities such as house warmings, box suppers, lyceum programs, birthday and wedding parties, and numerous other get-togethers. People were no longer forced to find their recreation and entertainment in their own back yards and friendships were made with people who, few short years before, were almost total strangers.

Our increasing mobility was reflected in other ways as more social notices and advertisements of coming community events appeared in the weekly *Sumatra Record* and young people especially thronged to the place "where the action was." Maybe it was to Ingomar or Melstone to a dance or movie or possibly to Forsyth or Roundup to some special attraction that came to the area only once a year. Wherever it was it wasn't too far to travel in the latest sedan with a throw-back top and celluloid curtains to be hastily put up when rain threatened.

More news briefs in the local newspaper described inter-family visits, usually taking place on weekends: "Mr. & Mrs. D. Van Rowland and family of the Blacktail community entertained Dr. and Mrs. J.E. Midgett and their four children at their farm Sunday after church services in the local school building. The Roland's daughter, Leona, and her husband, Joe Bernhard, and their year old baby were also present. Mrs. Midgett reports they had a very nice turkey dinner with all the trimmings and that she enjoyed seeing the Rowland place again as she hadn't been out there since a Red Cross meeting during the war period."

Another typical example: "Paul McDonald and Claire Ballard, two local Beau Brummels, took their girl friends, the Hayes sisters, Thelma and Aline, for a ride to Musselshell Friday night to attend the commencement exercises and dance that followed. One of the sweet girl graduates was an old acquaintance of the local belles." Or it might have been: "The Bert Dorsh family from the south country returned from a week's stay in Butte Saturday on No. 18. The Dorshes were formerly connected with an egg and poultry concern in the big town and Bert says that the trip was a combination social and business visit with some of his relations in the Mining City."

Such railroad trips could be made easily due to the convenient schedule of the trains through Sumatra. Trains No. 18 eastbound and No. 17 westbound stopped at the local station at 8:10 AM and 11:17 PM, respectively, so trips east to Forsyth and Miles City for shopping or taking care of county business could easily be made in one day. Trips west were not so convenient as Trains No. 15 and 16 were the fast trains and did not stop at the smaller towns except by flag and then only in case of emergency or passengers going a hundred miles or more.

I think few people living in the little towns like Sumatra and others similarly situated realized the effect these developments in transportation facilities were having on the continued growth of their communities. For the first six or eight years of its existence Sumatra had gradually grown in both population and the number and variety of businesses required to supply the needs of the surrounding settlers. By 1918 homesteading days in Montana and especially Rosebud County were nearly over. Most of the basic needs such as lumber and other building materials, fencing supplies, and farm machinery were pretty well supplied. As a result the two lumber yards and Tom Brown's farm implement business were feeling the effects of reduced demand for their products.

This condition was only aggravated by the changes in transportation patterns. Many people, both in town and the rural areas, could now make overnight trips to the larger trade centers such as Forsyth, Roundup, Miles City, Lewistown, and even Billings, where they could choose from a much greater stock of goods at considerably lower prices than they were charged in the small towns. This situation, combined with a gradual decrease in population due to the war and the continuing drought, had a definitely harmful effect on business conditions for the merchants of Sumatra.

By 1919 nearly everyone in the little community, whether farmer, rancher, businessman, or banker, was beginning to feel the squeeze, and rumor had it that some business houses would soon close their doors. The publisher of the *Sumatra Record*, Henry Poll, was one of the first to leave when, in 1919, he sold his print shop and equipment to E.F. McRae who had formerly edited a small weekly paper at Tindall, one of the little settlements in the north country. About the same time Harry Jaffe apparently read the handwriting on the wall and sold his store to a Mr. McInaney, who stayed in business a little over a year. The Jaffes moved to Roundup and later to the west coast.

The partnership of Dick Imhoff and Ben Carlen in their general store established in 1915 had lasted only a couple of years before they could see it would not provide an ample living for both of them and their young families. Dick continued the business until late 1921 or early 1922 when Art Over and Claire Ballard bought him out. Two hotels in the little town were one too many and management changed hands often but none of their proprietors could make a good living. Transportation improvements only worsened this situation and many names—Hayes, Holmes, King, McDonald, Krause, Carmichael, Herbold—were associated at one time or another with the hotel business until both buildings burned to the ground in 1928.

Despite the unfavorable conditions from 1918 to 1920 many businessmen seemed to maintain their faith in the country and decided to weather it out. Tom Brown invested in a new building in 1918 for his farm machinery dealership and early in the twenties went into the garage business in competition with Mrs. Bartlett. About the same time a Mr. Dahl built a small lumber yard a block east of Main Street. Shortly afterward the Yellowstone Lumber Co., closed its yard and moved out. The business exodus had begun but was still less than flight until the mid-twenties.

Even the Milwaukee railroad through this part of Montana began to feel the effects of the downturn in freight traffic and the big depot warehouse that had been nearly full of commodities of all kinds was now half empty. With production declining fewer cars of grain were being loaded at the elevator. Despite an increase of cattle raising on some ranches, especially in the north country, loadings from the stockyard at Sumatra gradually dropped, in part because more stockmen were hauling their cattle to local markets by truck.

All in all, the business trend was downward and by 1919 and 1920 everybody in eastern Montana had been affected. The change was so gradual that most people of the Sumatra community were either unaware of the seriousness of the situation or refused to believe it would last more than a year or two. In either case there was likely very little that could have been done to halt the downward spiral or improve the plight of people in western Rosebud county. If they had realized the gravity of their predicament the exodus would probably only have been much earlier and more general than it eventually became.

Chapter IX

Despite a dearth of snowfall during the winter of 1918-19 and the threat of a short crop at the end of the following summer we enjoyed a better than fair year. Even though some settlers were beginning to get a bit fidgety and public auction sales were being advertised at the rate of two or three a month, I don't think the folks gave much thought to the possibility of pulling stakes and giving up everything they had worked so hard for almost five years.

With the war over most of the boys had been mustered out of the service by March or April 1919 but many had decided not to return to their previous homes. A few came back to Sumatra long enough to dispose of their property, while others went directly to new jobs either in the more populous areas of the state or back to their original homes. It was estimated that Montana lost over two thousand of its young men either on the war's mortality lists or as disillusioned discharged doughboys who found it difficult to adjust to the post-war world they found in the state in 1919 and 1920.

This situation only aggravated and retarded the general welfare and development of all of Montana and especially the sparsely populated eastern part of the state. With little industry and an almost total dependence on farming and ranching for its growth, the loss of population only added to the problems created by the drought conditions and the general decrease in farm production and income of the region. A backward glance at these and other contemporary conditions of the period explains, at least partially, the whys and wherefores accounting for the gradual decadence of western Rosebud County over the next ten years.

Despite these distinct signs of the times, the Midgetts seemed to escape any serious effects during the next two years through 1920. In fact a number of things happened in 1919 that counted on the plus side as far as our happiness and welfare were concerned. The first and probably the most important as far as it affected Dad was the unexpected replacement of the old Model T. Hard usage for a variety of purposes over a period of more than six years, mostly on Montana roads and trails, had brought the old girl to the place where she was held together with bailing wire and tape and we expected her to "give up the ghost" most any day. More and more difficult to start and with parts falling off on practically every trip, the car was no longer dependable transportation. In fact, a year earlier the body, which had become rather dilapidated, had been replaced by an Overland car body given to Dad by Mr. Bartlett whom he had treated during his fatal illness. His brother, George, did the mechanical work in the exchange.

From the beginning of his practice at Sumatra Dad had made arrangements with the hospital in Miles City, headed by Dr. Garberson, to take care of any surgical cases too serious or complicated for him to handle. During the winter of 1918-19 the surgeon had, by way of the grapevine, learned of the Midgett's transportation troubles. This is Dad's version of what happened a few months later:

"On the morning of April first I was summoned to the railroad station where an emergency telephone call was awaiting me. Upon answering the phone I heard Dr. Garberson on the other end of the line urging me to take the next train to Miles City but he said he could not take time on the railroad phone to explain the situation in detail. Believing it probably pertained to a patient I had taken to the hospital about a week earlier I agreed to take Milwaukee train No. 16 that evening and arrived in Miles City about eleven o'clock.

"Dr. Garberson met me at the station, but instead of going directly to the hospital he drove straight to his home because, the doctor explained, it was too late in the day to do anything about the situation. The next morning only added to the mystery of the situation when my host did not seem to be in any hurry about making any move and said nothing about the supposed case. After eating breakfast he asked me to come with him saying he had something he wanted to show me. We walked together out to the garage behind the house and Dr. Garberson opened the door. Pointing to a very well-kept 1917 Model T he asked me how I liked it. Before I could reply, the doctor said, 'That is yours.' Of course I was struck dumb and minutes passed before I realized what was happening or could say anything in appreciation for my good fortune."

It turned out Dr. Garberson had recently purchased a larger car but instead of trading in the Ford, he had decided to give it to the Midgetts. Imagine the family's surprise late that evening when Dad drove into the back yard in Tin Lizzie No. 2 having covered the hundred miles from Miles City to Sumatra in record time.

And about the patient in the hospital? He had recovered nicely and had gone home the day before. The long and short of this little episode was we had dependable transportation again. But more important was that an expected expense of at least $800 had been eliminated from Dad's budget for 1919. Dad said it was the nicest April Fool joke ever played on him.

In the spring of the same year we had the pleasure of welcoming two new neighbors whose homes were built on lots adjoining our place, one on the south side and the other across the alley to the west. To make it enjoyable they were both close relatives; Dad's brother, Jim with his wife, Millie, and Mother's sister-in-law, Myrtle Fox. Both had emigrated to Sumatra from the same area in Illinois we had left five years earlier. For the next two years Uncle Jim, who had been a farmer all his life, helped out with the work on the ranch and we managed to raise enough of a crop to enable Dad to keep up his payments on the place.

Aunt Myrtle had divorced her husband, Lawrence Fox, Mother's step-brother, in 1918 and had a little boy, Robert, about two years old. She had taken some training in practical nursing a few years earlier and after the divorce she wrote Mother expressing a desire to get away from the old home haunts. Again the wheels in Dad's head started turning and the result was an invitation to her to come to Sumatra to help set up a maternity home that he would help her build. Primarily it was to serve as a place to which expectant mothers living in the outlying areas could come for prenatal care and the birth of their babies. By autumn, 1919, the place was ready for business and for the next five or six years it was well patronized, with patients making reservations from as far as 50 to 100 miles away.

I am not clear about the rates for the services rendered but I believe Aunt Myrtle never charged more than three dollars per day, and the whole job, prenatal care, delivery, and postnatal care, was covered by Dad's single fee of about $35. It wasn't much of a financial burden to have children in those days and most families were quite large. Two babies I can remember being born in the new facility were Don Davis, who now lives in Missoula, Montana, and Bill Dutton who is a rancher in the Jordan-Sand Springs area. Years later, when the folks left Sumatra, between 40 and 50 new arrivals had begun their lives in the Midgett-Fox Maternity Home.

*   *   *   *

The first Fourth of July celebration in the area since 1915 was held at Sumatra in the summer of 1919. Approximately 1,000 people from miles around crowded the main street and the still undeveloped park area of the little town. Since there were no trees in the "park" all the activities of the celebration were held right out in the July sun of a hot, dry summer day in eastern Montana. A number of common pastimes—horseshoes, croquet, and volleyball—had been set up for the enjoyment of those who liked to actively participate, especially the younger people.

Serving tables were set up in a square formation in the middle of the block with the ladies of the village serving home-cured ham sandwiches, baked beans, potato salad, coffee and pop, all furnished by the businessmen. Moving around the tables, the crowds filled their paper plates, then spread their blankets on any level space they could find in the very limited shade and spent the next two hours renewing old friendships with neighbors sometimes not seen for many months. Many of the big crowd went back for seconds and Dad gave the youngsters of grade school age and under ice cream cones from his soda fountain.

Following the clearing away of the small amount of remaining food, the serving tables were disassembled and moved away leaving room for the games and contests arranged for the entertainment of the crowd. The program started with foot races of many kinds for a half dozen age groups. As many as 12 or 15 contestants vied for prizes of money, ribbons, and candy bars. A tug-of-war between ten farmers north of town and a like number to the south resulted in a victory for the northerners after a terrific struggle. All the participants desiring a little refresher after the battle were treated to a beer at Cotton Duff's saloon.

About four o'clock most of the crowd moved south across the railroad for the pièce-de-résistance of the day, the first local baseball game since the U.S. had entered the war. A few days earlier a new diamond had been scraped out of sagebrush-covered gumbo hardpan that had seen very little rain for nearly two months. Our neighboring village, Melstone, furnished the opposition for our young team. They came to town confident, with a couple of victories under their belts, largely due to the pitching of forty-year-old Doctor Crouse, who had seen some semipro experience before coming to Melstone. However, they failed to reckon with a young ex-service man by the name of Claire Ballard who came up from Vananda to pitch for the Sumatra nine.

Our lineup included Charley Plumb, catcher; Bob Ross, 2nd base; Lou Jacobson, 1st base; Bill Morris, 3rd base; Vic Morris, shortstop. One of the Finch boys—Dave, I think—Henry Thayer, and I completed the starting lineup at the outfield positions. The visitors brought an umpire who worked behind the bat and Dad made the decisions on the bases. Since the local team was playing its first game, only two or three had baseball uniforms or shoes, so we didn't make a very professional appearance.

It was a pitcher's duel from start to finish with neither team able to garner a hit for the first four innings. Three walks put two Melstone and one Sumatra runners on first base but none of them got any farther. Two hits and a walk off Ballard in the fifth produced a run for the visitors but the home team retaliated in the sixth when Charley Plumb hoisted one of Doc Crouse's curves over the outfielders' heads with Bob Ross on base and we had a 2-1 lead. Neither team could score in the last three innings and the long busy day ended on a joyous winning note for Sumatra and her people.

The happy mood of the crowd was given a boost when, during the afternoon, a heavy bank of dark clouds appeared in the western sky. By 5 P.M. quite a few families living some distance away had left for home to avoid the sticky gumbo roads that always followed a rain. The storm broke a few minutes after the game and almost a half-inch of water fell in less than half an hour. Although the drought had not been completely broken, enough moisture fell to green up the grain fields and helped greatly to fill out the heads of wheat. Later reports indicated that the storm was quite general in the dryland area of western Rosebud County. No hail was reported.

I would be remiss if I didn't confess that, although it wasn't exactly planned, the day's celebration turned out to be a nice windfall for the Midgetts. Being the only place in town handling ice cream and soft drinks, the drug store was the center of activity for hundreds of the holiday visitors who felt the need to slake their thirsts or enjoy a little refreshment on that hot summer day. Although the stores closed at noon, Dad had provided for these needs by constructing a counter across both ends of the drug store's front porch where we could provide ice cream and pop. At the prevailing price of a nickel for a cone or a bottle of orange, rootbeer, or Coca Cola it took a lot of customers to pile up a very large heap of coins.

Imagine our surprise the next morning when a check of the previous day's sales revealed total receipts of more than $150 from the sale of 50 gallons of ice cream and 25 cases of pop. We worked hard to achieve such a one-day record in store income and it looked very good compared with the 15 to 20 dollars in normal daily receipts. Since approximately 30 percent of fountain receipts was profit there was more than 40 dollars that could apply to Dad's indebtedness. He must have been thankful for it even though it wasn't a large sum of money.

*   *   *   *

Early in August we enjoyed an unusual surprise when Dad received a letter telling us Grandfather Midgett would be leaving Flat Rock soon on the long train trip to Sumatra for a week's visit with us and Uncle Jim. He was nearly seventy years of age, a little old for such a journey, so Uncle Albert who lived in the nearby town of Robinson, accompanied him as far as Chicago and put him on the Milwaukee train headed for Montana.

After a couple of days rest Grandpa, Uncle Jim, Dad, my brother Robert, and I took the sixty mile trip north to Cat Creek via the county dirt road along the west bank of the Musselshell. This was the site of one of the first proven oil fields in Montana, discovered only a few months earlier. Although commercial production in the tract did not start for another year, 15 or 20 drilling sites had already been located in an area about five miles square. (By the late 1950s this field had produced more than 19,000,000 barrels of oil before its yield began to show a decrease indicating its drying up.)

A thunder shower came up early in the afternoon producing a very slick surface on the unimproved clay and gumbo roads. Before starting for home about three o'clock we dug out our tire chains and put them on. Despite these precautions we did a lot of slipping and sliding and had considerable difficulty climbing three or four of the low hills before we reached the state road fifteen miles from home. It took us almost five hours to make the sixty miles and we were happy to see the little town as we topped the last ridge two miles from home. As usual, Mother and Aunt Millie had a nice hot dinner waiting for us.

During the next few days we made trips westward up the Musselshell as far as Roundup and to Forsyth to the east. Grandpa was quite impressed with Montana and stated quite a few times that he wished he were a young man again so he could emigrate to the state. The weather cooperated while he was here so we got to see a lot of the country.

*   *   *   *

The summer of 1919 was climatically pretty much a replica of 1918. The light winter snowfall coupled with a renewed absence of soaking rains throughout eastern Montana in May and June contributed to the continuation of drought conditions and short crops by harvest time. Although some farmers began to diversify their crops to compensate for the drier conditions, the newly planted flax and barley failed to improve the agricultural economy even though market prices held.

As the months passed and the year moved inexorably toward winter, more and more "FOR SALE" signs were visible along the roads, and almost every week there was at least one or two auction sales advertised in the *Sumatra Record*. Despite all the bad omens most area dwellers continued to maintain their confidence that the country would soon return to more prosperous days.

Quite a few farmers in the area began to realize that, with the decrease in cash money from short grain crops, they had to find some other way to raise money to live on and pay their bills. A few went more heavily into beef cattle while others bought a small band of sheep and hoped to raise enough wool to sell at the high market prices. Probably the majority turned to increasing and up-grading their dairy herds and the production of milk and cream as a secondary crop.

Thousands of acres of the short grain harvest were mowed and stacked for feed that fall while many of the larger beef herds were greatly reduced when at least half of them were shipped to the St. Paul markets. Milk and cream were shipped directly to Miles City Creamery once a week in five and ten gallon cans and the farmers received their checks and empty cans by return express. Good prices for dairy products, meant milk turned out to be the "bread and butter" for many families during the winter of 1919-20.

*   *   *   *

The Rosebud County Fair was held in Forsyth late in August after being canceled for the two war years of 1917 and 1918. Since we now had dependable transportation, Dad decided to take the family on its first overnight trip since we had arrived in Montana. Even though crops in the drylands of the county were short, fairgoers compared the number and quality of the farm exhibits favorably with previous years. Most of them came from the Yellowstone River valley and the irrigated areas that comprised only a few thousand acres. Needless to say, we all had a wonderful time riding on the merry-go-round, Ferris wheel, and the pony rides, the big attractions in those days. Horse races, including a chariot race, and a few bucking horse events made up most of the program that ran until well after six o'clock. Dad won a doll by ringing the bell at the top of a pole by hitting a block of wood with a heavy sledge.

There were no flood lights at the fairgrounds in those days so there was no night program. Dad was a little leery about trying to drive home since there would be no help available on the way should we have a flat tire or a breakdown—quite common on Model Ts. He had written to the Commercial Hotel in Forsyth for reservations for the night and after a bowl of soup, a sandwich, and milk or coffee at the restaurant, we were all glad to hit the hay about 9:00 PM. We were up early the next morning and, after paying for our rooms—three dollars for the six of us—Mother bought a few articles of food we could eat on the road. We arrived home about noon Saturday after a pleasant trip with no troubles of any kind.

On our return Dad was greeted by waiting patients as he stepped out of the car. The first needing attention was John Ducummon who lived about twelve miles southwest of Sumatra on what was known as "The Bench." He had been brought to town by Claude Gray, a neighbor, an hour or so earlier after being struck by a rattlesnake while working in his field that morning. He was a very sick man and Aunt Myrtle had already put him to bed in one of the rooms upstairs in our home. Dad took his scalpel and cut open the wound. He then applied a vacuum cup to draw out the poison and wrapped the wound in a potassium permanganate poultice to counteract the poison. With no penicillins, antibiotics or sulfanilamides to act quickly in such cases Mr. Ducummon remained very ill for nearly a week with his leg badly swollen and turning black and blue as the days went by. He was out of his head for nearly three days before his recovery was certain.

The second case awaiting Dad was one of his expectant mothers at the maternity home. Labor had started two or three days earlier than expected and it was nip and tuck between the two patients until nearly six o'clock when a little boy baby made his appearance. The third case was a previous patient who had had a relapse but was not considered to be in serious condition. Dad had sent out some medicine to reduce the fever and temporarily relieve any pain until he could get out to see her, finally at about eight o'clock that night. She was feeling much better when he arrived and within a few days her recovery was complete. I wonder if Dad thought about the number of hours he had been working when he finally crawled in beside my Mother that night. A pleasant family outing was not without its price.

*   *   *   *

In 1918 my most serious teenage romance had begun when the Douglas Yates family moved in town to put their four children in school. Two of the boys, Corliss and Curtis, were in the lower grades and Velma was in the eighth grade. The older daughter, Ferrol, was starting high school after graduating two or three years earlier from the country school in their vicinity south of Sumatra. Although she was a year or so older than I, we were quite attracted to each other from first sight and for the next two years we hit it off to the exclusion of any other possible beaus or girl friends.

One night in the spring of 1920 especially sticks in my memory. I had gone down to Ferrol's home to study with her. The rest of her family had gone to bed when someone knocked on the front door. Ferrol opened it and to our surprise my Mother, who had decided I was a little late getting home, stood there. Looking at the time we discovered it was almost eleven o'clock. Suffice to say, it didn't happen again. I was only lucky Dad wasn't at home that night.

When Mr. Yates decided in 1920 to move his family to Miles City to work for the railroad company it was quite a blow, but it didn't end there. Every three or four weeks during the summer I used Dad's railroad pass to make the trip to Miles City, going down on No. 18 on Saturday morning and coming home on No. 17 Sunday night. When I went away to college in late August we were just as thick as ever but during the year the affair seemed to cool off a little. In the summer of 1921 I still made two or three trips to Miles City, but it never was the same and we agreed that, except for a few letters during the year, the romance was over and we never saw each other again. I never knew whether or not she ever married and I guess her interest in my later life ceased from 1921 on.

Chapter X

By 1919 most of the tarpaper shacks, dugouts, and sod-covered shelters of the homesteaders of the 1912-1915 era in eastern Montana had disappeared from the great expanse of sage brush, cactus and Russian thistle. Many homesteaders who found the going too tough had literally walked away from their humble abodes relinquishing their rights back to Uncle Sam or turning them over to the county in lieu of delinquent tax payments. In either case, they called it quits and pulled out for parts unknown hoping their situations would change for the better by some good fortune.

Others, probably more fortunate in their choice of land and wiser or more diligent in its use, had prospered during their four or five years and had improved their living conditions. Two-story frame houses, large barns and other substantial farm buildings replaced the original structures of their early homestead days. Hopes remained high among these people that the area around Sumatra would return to the prosperity it had enjoyed from 1912 to 1917.

However, by 1920, after two years of unfavorable weather accompanied by such afflictions as insect invasions, hail, and dust storms, even the newer farm homes were being abandoned when their owners found it increasingly difficult to meet their financial obligations. A few places were sold to new owners coming into the area for the first time while others were bought up by neighbors who needed more acreage for expanded operations.

Many surviving homesteads in the Sumatra area were heavily mortgaged to the local bank that, like most small institutions in eastern Montana, had been more than liberal in making farm and real estate loans to their clients when times were good. With changed conditions repayment of their obligations, including those to the bank, were increasingly difficult for many of the borrowers. Reserves had gradually dwindled and, despite assistance from the larger members of the bank chain, liquid assets grew scarcer for the smaller banks like Sumatra State.

The continued poor growing conditions were accompanied by a growing feeling of pessimism permeating the area. Many people, like my folks, stubbornly maintained their faith in the country and refused to admit defeat. But liquidation time had arrived for many and bank foreclosures became frequent. Numerous auction sale advertisements appeared in the *Sumatra Record* and the *Forsyth Independent*. Most of these sales were held under the auspices of the bank that held the paper (mortgages or promissory notes) and Bob Ross's name often appeared on the ads as clerk of the sale. In most cases this meant the bank got its money first and the owner kept any remainder. Thus, many families left the Sumatra area with almost nothing except the clothes on their backs and a few household articles packed in a dilapidated open touring car or light truck.

During the next two or three years (1920-1923) bidding on auctioned household goods, farm machinery, and livestock continued brisk and prices were attractive as people from miles around attended sales hoping to pick up bargains. By 1923, however, used farm machinery had become a drag on the market in eastern Montana and, in some instances, purchasers who bid them in no longer moved them off the abandoned farms. Scores of little-used plows, discs, harrows, and cultivators were left out to rust away. By 1925 a casual trip around the countryside revealed a growing number of tractors and even a few thresher separators in fields where they had harvested what turned out to be the last grain crops ever to be grown on this once promising land.

*   *   *   *

Despite the general deterioration of growing conditions in eastern Montana from 1918 on, the population of the area around Sumatra remained stable for the next few years. Although there was a decrease in the number of pupils in the surrounding rural schools, the enrollment in both the grade and high school at Sumatra continued to grow when some of the farm residents moved into town for the winter. There was only one other high school, Musselshell, between Roundup and Forsyth and Sumatra was accessible to the pupils in the north country who were graduating from the eighth grade.

By fall 1919 interest in the high school at Sumatra had grown so rapidly that there were more students than could be accommodated in the little town's homes. Since there were no school busses to transport them, students living more than five or six miles from school usually made arrangements to stay with families in town from Monday through Friday and their folks took them home for the weekend. Others whose homes were as many as 50 to 75 miles away went home only for the holidays.

In an effort to take care of the overflow during the ensuing school year the school board decided to rent a couple of private homes as temporary living quarters. Since Uncle Jim and Aunt Millie had no children they opened up their home and acted as house parents to six or eight boys. The Charley Plumb family of four moved out of their home and a house mother was hired to take care of about the same number of girls. Meals were served in a dining room in the basement of the school where Mrs. D.W. Payton, the cook, lived with her daughter, Lola Davis.

The school year 1919-20 was the most active and exciting of all the six years the Midgetts had lived in Montana. There was now a full four-year curriculum with the addition of a freshman class of twelve to fifteen new students. There was no change in the junior and senior classes but three new sophomores boosted the total enrollment to approximately thirty.

Along with the growth of the student body came an increase in the number of both boys and girls who were interested in basketball. Those few who had learned a little about the fundamentals in Jaffe's warehouse the winter before used their meager knowledge to help the new candidates for both teams. Under the direction of Prof. Emil Peterson, the new principal, we began to take on the appearance of basketball teams by the first of December.

Both teams consisted mainly of freshmen and sophomores as I was the only senior boy and none of the three senior and junior girls went out for basketball. Tony Schleder and I played forward positions, Bill Dirrim was our center, and Ralph Jones and Harley

Mockerman were the guards. Bill Schleder, a sophomore, and two freshmen, Ray Jones and Roy Hoagland, were our reserves.

The girls' team included Myrtle Smith, Anna Whitney, Lois Booker, Mamie Horton, and my sister Elizabeth, all sophomores, and freshmen Bernice Rowland, Henrietta Schleder, Marguerite Cody, and Mabel Metzel. The last-named three were all rather husky girls and did a good job of terrorizing their opponents in most of their games. In fact, when we boys scrimmaged against the girls in practice we often came off second best. I, with my 129 pounds, often looked to big Bill Dirrim, 170 pounds, for protection from the Amazons.

In those days girls' games were played on a divided court with six girls, the center and forwards playing on one half and three guards on the other. Girls' basketball was as popular as boys' and every small school's schedule provided for double-headers. Nobody even considered that basketball might be too arduous physically for the "gentler" sex.

Our schedule consisted of seven double-headers, home and home, with the high schools at Rosebud, Forsyth, Musselshell, Lavina, Ryegate, Klein and Roundup, all towns along the Milwaukee railroad. This made it possible to ride the trains, thereby eliminating cold auto trips on icy, rough roads and the chance of being caught in the blizzards that often hit the country between mid-November and mid-March.

Going west we rode on train No. 15, the Olympian, by special permission of the railroad superintendent. Leaving on Friday morning we returned Sunday on No. 18, the Columbian, after playing double headers on successive nights. Going east to Rosebud or Forsyth we left on No. 18, played only one double header, and returned on No. 15 the next morning. The experience of staying at hotels overnight and eating at restaurants (not cafes) was a new one for us and we enjoyed it almost as much as playing the games.

Our biggest problem was the lack of a building large enough to play our home games. Since the school building did not contain a gymnasium and no edifice such as a lodge room or public hall existed in Sumatra, it appeared our dreams of playing basketball during the 1919-20 season would be only that. This was dispelled, however, when in the spring of 1919 Tom Brown proposed to the school board a plan to add a second story to the new farm implement store that he was building just west of the Imhoff-Carlen store. The board agreed to lease the upstairs for practice and games and other school activities during the year. Although quite small for a basketball court we managed to make it do for a couple of years until a new dormitory-gymnasium was constructed.

Spectators at games stood along the sides or sat on benches across the south end of the floor. With only a fifteen foot ceiling it was almost impossible to shoot baskets from very far out on the floor. The only door to the upper floor was located at the top of an outside stairway at the northeast corner of the building. The inside space was limited even more by a large jacketed coal stove in the southeast corner. I often wondered what the people crowded into that room would have done if a fire had broken out in the building. With no water supply or even a fire extinguisher, the result would have been nothing short of disaster.

With only three substitutes available on the boys' team we could not afford to foul out often. However, the game of basketball in those days was regarded as a non-contact sport and even though we were allowed only four fouls each it was seldom a player exceeded the limit and had to leave the game. Ten team fouls were regarded as a lot of violations but I believe the game was just as exciting as it is now with all the blocks, screens, picks, and other maneuvers that only add to an excessive amount of contact in today's game.

There were no classifications of schools as there are now. All except the ten or twelve larger schools in Montana scheduled games with any others they wished to play and usually didn't travel over 50 to 60 miles. There was no Montana High School Association to ride herd over all secondary school activities, make up schedules, supervise tournament play, and assign all the game officials who today are required to pass exams on the rules before they can wear the striped shirt and blow a whistle. A half century ago we were lucky to find someone within twenty miles who knew enough about the rules to even try to officiate a game and occasionally the two coaches refereed their own games. We never had more than one official and he often handled both the boys' and girls' games plus a third game played by town teams, all for the big sum of $5 or less.

As we now had a place to play, a number of the young men of the community organized an independent team and practiced twice a week with the school team. This opposition helped us a great deal since we did not have enough players to scrimmage with full teams. Some of the young fellows who made up the team were the two Morris boys, Vic and Bill, Henry Thayer, Dave Finch, and even Dad who was then about 45 years old. When they played other town teams following the high school games, two or three of us school boys substituted in the second half and played a quarter or two. Suffice it to say we were ready to hit the hay by the time we got home. Since we had no showers or change rooms we had to pull on a shirt and pants over our uniforms and hurry home before we "took our death" of colds. I guess we must have been a hardy bunch as I can't remember any of our players missing a game because of illness.

That first year both boys' and girls' uniforms were homemade and would be regarded as quite primitive compared to the fancy ones players wear nowadays. The boys wore ordinary undershirts without sleeves and the pants were cut-off khaki trousers. After dyeing the shirts black, orange felt numbers were sewn on the back and a block S on the front. We wore black long sox rolled under the knees and an ordinary pair of white tennis shoes.

The girls' uniform consisted of orange colored middy blouses with full black bloomers--the fashion for girl athletes of the time. We made quite a pretty picture but it didn't seem to affect our play. We had no such fancy gear as warm-up suits so we wore our own sweaters or jackets before the games and when we were on the bench.

In this, our first year of interscholastic competition, we boys earned the right to go to the district tournament at Forsyth by winning nine of our fourteen games, six at home and three away. In tournament play we won over Hysham but lost to Forsyth and Roundup. Overall we were very well satisfied with the results of our first season's play.

The girls also had a successful season but there was no tournament for them then.

In addition to the basketball games, which were attended by nearly everyone in the community, other recreation was provided by public dances on Saturday nights after the games or in the country school houses scattered around northwestern Rosebud County. Box suppers at midnight were often put on as benefits for various groups such as the Catholic Ladies, PTA, the town baseball team and others who found it an easy way to raise a little money for a good cause.

The women prepared box lunches that were auctioned by number to the highest male bidder who usually could not identify the owner of the box until after he had bought it. This was a good mixer as the lady who prepared the lunch ate with its lucky bidder, and quite often they were total strangers meeting for the first time. Sometimes some ill feeling developed when budding romances were put to the test as rivals outbid each other or were mistaken in their efforts to recognize their girlfriend's lunch box. But mostly it all added to the merriment of the occasion and ended up with no bodily harm to the participants. Often the sum of a hundred dollars or more was realized from the event and worthy organizations were helped to provide needed equipment or services. Our town baseball team was able to purchase all its bats, balls, and catcher's mitt with the proceeds received from such an event in the spring of 1920.

*   *   *   *

During the 1919-20 school year numerous inquiries were received by the Sumatra school board regarding the high school from people as much as 75 miles away in all directions. Requests for information regarding living accommodations, the cost of room and board, and the extent of the curriculum offered came from Ingomar, Melstone, the residents of the north country, and even as far south as Ashland and Birney in the southern part of Rosebud County. By early 1920 all signs pointed to the probability of an increase of 25 to 30 new students if living quarters could be provided. In an effort to take care of the situation the board decided to do three things: arrange to rent more temporary housing for the girls, bring in an unused rural school building in which to house six or eight boys, and start working on plans for a new combination dormitory-gymnasium to be completed by the fall of 1921.

Because I planned to go away to school in August 1920, the folks rented my room and two others upstairs to some of the girls. They ate breakfast with the Midgetts but the other two meals were taken at the school dining room. This made some extra work for my Mother even though the girls helped some with chores around the house by keeping their room clean and doing their own laundry.

The plans for the new building were drawn up by the same architect who had done the work on the new school in 1915-16, and in fall 1920 a bond issue for $25,000 was passed by the voters in the district. Most of the excavation was completed before cold weather set in but construction was not started until spring. Work was rushed on the building during the summer and, although it was not completed when school opened, the dormitory portion was ready for occupancy early in November 1921. The gym, not quite finished, was ready for basketball practice right after Thanksgiving.

In addition to a kitchen-dining complex and four student rooms downstairs there were eight more rooms on the second floor. The gymnasium formed a T across the back or west end of the dormitory and the entire building was lighted by electricity from a small gasoline-powered generator. Although the brightness varied with the pulsation of the motor, spectators soon became accustomed to the flicker of the lights. This was the first building in Sumatra to have electric lights and certainly was a wonderful improvement over the gas mantle lamps in most homes and business buildings. Heat was provided by a hot air furnace with outlets in the floors of the rooms.

The dormitory project proved to be a good idea for all the rooms were reserved before the building was completed. New students came from miles around and some I can remember were the Batson sisters, Florence and Alice, and Sarah Spang from Lame Deer, the Scott brothers from the Edwards vicinity, and Jim Bowman from the Tindall country north of Sumatra.

The cost of room and board was kept to a very reasonable 35 to 40 dollars a month and the experiment was a complete success from its beginning. The net receipts derived from it plus the student tuition from other school districts made it possible to redeem the 20-year construction bonds long before they matured in 1940. As John Dorsh wrote in the 1923 annual, "Each year sees a larger number of names on the register of the high school and it is due chiefly to the dormitory." This was true even during the drought years, 1920-1925, when many area residents were leaving the country and school population generally experienced a sharp decline. During those years the graduating class grew from three in 1920 to a maximum of twenty in 1926. The total enrollment in Sumatra High School rose to approximately 75 students in the latter year.

*   *   *   *

With the approach of colder weather in the fall of 1919 I was hired by the board to fire the school furnace every weekday morning. Uncle Jim did all the janitor and necessary service work in the school as well as carrying out the ashes and banking the fire at night. I was paid about 25 dollars a month for the winter months and the job was only one of the four or five ways by which I earned money to go on to college in 1920.

When the United States entered World War I in 1917 interest in world affairs and especially the war itself greatly increased among the general populace. This interest in current affairs definitely affected the people of the Sumatra community and, since the daily newspaper was the only source of up-to-date information, Dad and I decided to take on the agency for sale of the *Butte Miner*, Montana's largest daily newspaper.

Originally we ordered ten copies per day that were delivered on train No. 18 about 8:15 in the morning. I had five or six regular customers to whom I delivered a paper before going to school and the rest were sold in the drug store. As the country became more involved in the war the demand for papers grew and we increased the order to fifteen and then twenty. By the time the struggle ended we were also receiving a few copies of the *Billings Gazette* and the *Lewistown*

Democrat-News for customers who preferred them. At a profit of two cents a paper, I not only bought most of my own clothes but also started a small savings account.

Another source of income developed about the same time when, in 1918, I made an agreement with the Buzzard Photo Shop in Forsyth to act as their agent in Sumatra. I was paid a commission on all film and photo work left at the store to be forwarded to them by mail. They developed and printed all of my own films without charge so during the ensuing two years I kept my Brownie Kodak quite busy. The money realized from this little enterprise didn't make me rich but it did help me realize my hopes of continuing my education.

My fourth money-making project came about in the spring of 1920 when I happened to be in the right place at the right time. I have mentioned that, due to the unfavorable weather in eastern Montana, many farmers had diversified their efforts by substantially increasing their herds of milk cows and selling milk and cream to the Forsyth and Miles City Creameries.

Following a very good summer business in 1919 the owners of the latter company decided to set up a receiving station at Sumatra and hire a local manager to run it during the summer months. Since we purchased all our ice cream from them, Dad received a letter asking him to recommend someone for the job. He asked me if I thought I could handle it and, with little hesitation, I replied I was sure that I could.

Dad's recommendation apparently was enough and I was hired for the job to begin as soon as school was out about the middle of May 1920. The little house behind the drug store was empty so the Creamery rented it from Dad for 25 dollars a month and installed the testing machinery in the front part of it. From here I could also keep an eye on the store when I wasn't busy testing milk. After a couple of days training under a Creamery employee I started on my new job right after school was out. With a local station to test their milk and pay the farmers on the spot, business was even better than it had been during previous summers and, paid on a commission basis, I earned nearly two hundred dollars the first year.

The milk testing business turned out to be my main occupation for the next two summers after college let out. Betty and Dad, with Uncle Jim's help, took care of it during May. They gave the farmers two-day-a-week service which was stretched to three, Tuesday, Thursday, and Saturday, after the first of June. Despite the decrease in the farm population the amount of milk and cream shipped from the Sumatra station showed a steady increase. The dairy business took over as the cash producer for farmers as drought conditions worsened. By 1922 I was earning more than $300 for my summer's efforts that turned out to be a big factor in keeping me in college.

Chapter XI

Three consecutive years of hot dry summers and cold snowless winters had rapidly and surely turned eastern Montana back into a part of the "Great American Desert." This was especially true of our part of the country where water sources were far apart and irrigation was only a dream. By 1920 and 1921 the intense heat and lack of precipitation during the normal rainy season resulted in the gradual drying up of the few small reservoirs and water holes upon which the livestock depended. By the latter year the level of the water table in most of the region had dropped so low that many wells, fifty to a hundred feet deep, were going dry. Those who could began hauling water by tank trucks from the Musselshell, Missouri, and Yellowstone Rivers hoping fall rains would replenish their supply.

By late September 1921 it was evident Mother Nature was not cooperating. Many of those farmers who still maintained their faith in the area decided the only practical solution to their water problem was to construct small dams in the coulees and swales running through their places to catch the melting snow water in spring. The small reservoir on our place west of town had nearly dried up, and Dad and his renter decided this was a good time to clean out the silt that had partially filled it over the past five or six years. During that period it had served the purpose for which it had been constructed.

In addition to another short grain crop, the fourth in a row, farmers who had turned to cattle and sheep for supplementary income now found it necessary to market most of their livestock at least a year sooner than they had planned. With both water and feed shortages looming for the winter this was their only hope of reducing part of their impending losses and avoiding still deeper debt. For others it was too late and the only solution for them was to sell out and leave the country.

I did not realize the extent to which this was affecting our family and how Dad's situation was gradually becoming more serious as conditions deteriorated throughout the area. I am sure his financial problems showed very little if any improvement after 1919 when many of the clientele upon whom he was dependent for an income, either as patients or customers, were leaving the country.

Dad was no longer actively interested in the operation of the farm, now leased on a share basis, except to keep up annual payments on it. Unfavorable crop growing conditions and the decline in market prices for grain and livestock after the war reduced his share of the farm income, which could no longer provide a profit beyond his contracted obligations.

Even under such unfavorable conditions I believe as late as 1921 neither Dad nor Mom had seriously entertained the notion of leaving Sumatra and everything for which they had striven for seven years. In fact, at least as far as we kids were aware, the early '20s seemed to move along quite normally and happily for our family. We were busy people and I sometimes think with all our "busyness" we didn't have time to spend worrying about the condition of the country and the prospects for the future.

*   *   *   *

Some of the events in 1920 were of particular interest to the Midgett family because of our active participation in them. The first of these was the culmination of my twelve years of work and study when I finally became one third of the first graduating class of Sumatra High School. Even though it may sound a bit boastful, I was proud to be the only boy in the class of three and to give the first valedictory address in the history of the school. The other two members of the class, Gladys Williams and Elizabeth Schleder, became Mrs. Henry Kreider and Mrs. John Hecker within a year of their graduation. Both still live in the general area and, although widowed now, have raised quite large families, some of whom also live in the Sumatra area.

My principal ambition after graduation was to continue my education by enrolling in college that fall. I wrote to quite a few institutions of higher education and by June had received bulletins and curriculum schedules from a half dozen of them including the State College at Bozeman, the State University at Missoula, and

Montana Wesleyan College at Helena. Since the latter institution was denominational and the Methodist Church was one of its sponsors, Dad and Mom indicated a definite preference for me to go there from the very start.

The choice finally came a month or so later when, in the middle of July, a group of six of our Methodist young people, known as Epworth Leaguers, attended the first annual state-wide Institute at Luccock Park, about ten miles southeast of Livingston at the north end of the Absaroka Mountains. Those who made the trip included my sister, Elizabeth, and me, Myrtle Smith, Ralph Jones, Bill Dirrim, and Bernice Rowland. Bernice's father drove his big Franklin sedan and took the three girls and most of the luggage. I was happy to drive our new flivver with the other two boys, Rev. W.C. Smith, the new pastor at Forsyth, and the rest of the luggage, including food and camping supplies.

Where the money for the trip was coming from never seemed to be too much of a worry even though none of our parents had any spare funds. Other than a balance of about $25 in our League treasury and a few dollars each of us had saved, the money for Betty and me had to come from our folks. But, as usual, when money was needed for any worthy cause it seemed somehow to be available. I remember the morning we left when Dad came over to the side of the car and put two ten dollar bills in my hand along with the kindly admonition, "Don't waste it, son." Since we were taking most of our food with us there wasn't much to spend money on, so at the end of the trip I gave five dollars back to him. Most of our expenditures had gone for gasoline at 18 cents a gallon and a few quarts of oil.

The distance from Sumatra to the campground was about 225 miles, the longest trip any of us had ever taken by car. We started too late to make the entire distance in one day, and unfortunately, it had rained quite hard the night before in the southern part of the state. With most roads still either dirt or gravel, our progress was rather slow from Billings west and we were forced to stay overnight in our cars at Big Timber.

It was the first time that any of us had been in the mountains, which were very beautiful as they loomed up to the south and ahead of us as we approached Livingston. Later in the week more than half of the delegates had their first view of Yellowstone Park when we made the sixty mile journey to Gardiner and Mammoth Hot Springs. Other trips to Chico and Montanapolis Hot Springs gave many of us our first experience swimming in a warm water pool.

The week was one of great inspiration and wholesome recreation with almost every daylight hour filled with well-planned classes and recreation sessions. The friendships with the more than 200 young fellow-Methodists were not to be forgotten, some of them developing into much more than casual friendships over the next few years. It was there I made a firm decision to attend Montana Wesleyan in the fall. This was the outcome of many talks I had with the eight or ten delegates who were students at the school and a conference I had with Dr. Charles Donaldson, the college president, and other school officials. Their interest in me as a prospective student was flattering to say the least and nothing could have changed my mind after the "brain-washing" I received that week. Regardless, I have never been sorry I made that choice.

One incident of all the happenings of the week still sticks in my mind—the only unhappy occurrence of an otherwise enjoyable week. The final scheduled event on the last afternoon of the camp was a baseball game between the members of the clergy and a team composed of the "Instituters." Four innings of a very even game had passed when at the opening of the fifth I relieved our pitcher on the mound. For the next three innings the game continued close and then suddenly it happened.

Substitutions were frequent on both teams and at the beginning of the eighth inning one of the ministers went in to bat for a teammate. My second pitch to him went a little awry and struck him on the left temple. He dropped in his tracks and the game suddenly ended when all the players rushed to his aid. A quick trip to the hospital in Livingston revealed only a slight concussion and when I visited him the next morning I found him in good spirits and a forgiving mood. I saw him often in the next ten years and we became good friends even though there were more than thirty years difference in our ages.

Everybody was up by 5 AM the last morning. After dismantling our tents and packing our gear, we loaded our cars, ate a breakfast of ham and eggs, toast and coffee and bid a fond farewell to our newly made friends. We were on the road home by 6:30 and, after a brief stop at the hospital, we rolled along on Highway 10 (the Yellowstone Trail) at 25 or 30 miles per hour. With the exception of three or four gas and rest stops at the few service stations along the way, we made good time and pulled into home about 6 PM, a tired but happy bunch of teenagers.

  *   *   *   *

We didn't have long to wait for the third and probably most important event of 1920 for the Midgetts. It occurred five days after we arrived home from the Institute when, on the morning of the 25th of July we were awakened by gentle nudges from Dad who announced we now had a new baby sister, Phyllis Birdie. I believe her arrival was a complete surprise to all four of her older siblings and, although I was 17 years old, I was totally ignorant of the physical condition of my Mother previous to the arrival. The tradition of being born in my Mother's bed in her own home was broken when Phyllis made her appearance at Aunt Myrtle's Maternity Home, but it was still maintained when Dad officiated at her birth, the fifth time in our family history. The fact that the event was such a surprise indicates the naiveté and lack of sophistication of most of the youth of that period. Later, when I looked back on the few weeks before the baby's birth, I understood why my Mother wept one day when I answered her a little sharply when she asked me to do a little chore for her. Of course little Phyllis B was the instant darling of the whole family. I went away to school when she was only a little over a month old so we never got too well acquainted until I came home for the Christmas holidays. My Mother had shown her my picture quite a few times and, although only five months old, she seemed to recognize me.

  *   *   *   *

The month of June 1920 ushered in another summer of hot, dry weather. A total absence of spring rainfall, combined with hot winds and blazing sun bleached the pale greenness of the young grain fields and by mid-July little was left but stunted yellow stalks and discouragement. Even the natural grasses that, in better years, had been the source of abundant feed for horses, cattle, and sheep all year long, now dried up and turned brown. The livestock, in their hunger, began to roam from water hole to water hole in search of sustenance. By mid-August the Sumatra stock yards were filled with cattle and sheep in preparation for early shipment to market in an effort to save as much as possible of a losing cause. A byproduct of the drought conditions was the extreme danger of prairie fires especially along the railroad right-of-ways. Two remedies for the situation developed as conditions worsened during the summer. Farmers were hired to harvest the grass along the right-of-way and many of them cured and stored it for feed. This helped to relieve the hay situation for some farmers but only a comparative few could take advantage of it.

The other solution to the fire problem was a plan devised by the railroad to plow a fire guard just inside the right-of-way fences wherever the topography was level enough to allow it. The railroad superintendent hired Thad Bassett, the local delivery man and wholesale oil dealer, to do the work on a fifty mile stretch extending east and west of Sumatra. I can still see him hitching up his four horse team to an eight foot disc with spike-toothed harrow behind it. With the help of his two boys, Fred and Lynn, it took him more than two weeks to do the job. This operation greatly decreased the danger of any serious fires along the railroad during the late summer and early fall.

*   *   *   *

I left Sumatra early in September 1920 for Helena and enrolled for my freshman year at Montana Wesleyan College in a class of fifty to sixty students. Following my final decision in July to attend this school Dad made a trip to Helena in August and located a place for me to live and a part time job at Fischl's Drug Store across the street from the Northern Pacific depot. Morris Sanford, a freshman from Kalispell, and I decided to room together with a family by the name of Madden who lived six or seven blocks north of the college.

Both arrangements turned out to be rather short-lived. Morris took a part-time job as assistant physical director at the YMCA and decided to room there. My drug store job involved delivery of packages around towns to "customers" who seemed pleased with the service. It wasn't until later, after I had quit the job, that I learned I had been delivering bootleg liquor on some of these errands. However, that was not the reason I quit at the drug store, for I, with my 129 pounds had decided to go out for football, leaving no time for my job.

Morris invited me to move in with him and two other freshmen, Clarence Carlson and Kenneth Hammaker, in a large corner room at the Y that had just been vacated. I needed work to replace the drug store job and was lucky to land three furnace-firing jobs that paid me a total of 45 dollars a month. Late in October I added the janitorship at the Christian Church which paid a salary of 35 dollars a month. Eighty dollars a month in those times was pretty fair income for a college student so it more than paid for board and room. However my good fortune suddenly ended when I returned to Helena after my Christmas vacation at home and was informed my church job was "kaput" due to some laxness or mismanagement on the part of the student with whom I had made arrangements to care for it while I was gone.

Again Morris came to my rescue when he arranged for me to put in a few hours per week at the front desk at the Y. I was given my room for the time I spent there on Saturdays and Sundays and two or three weekday evenings. Morris and I ate most of our morning and evening meals at the Wise Cafe, about two blocks from the Y. We had our noon meal at Mills Hall, the girls' dormitory across 11th Avenue south of Main Hall, the only other building on campus.

Although I was a little on the light side for a football player and had no experience in the game I enjoyed working out with the squad and learned to take some hard knocks before the season was over. I always hoped to get into a game or two but Coach Allan Lemon didn't seem to see it that way. I assumed he just didn't want me to get hurt and was looking toward my making some contribution in future years. Regardless of his motive I stayed with it for the next three years and earned my letter as a senior as well as developing into a behemoth of 145 pounds.

Suffice it to say I greatly enjoyed my four years at Montana Wesleyan. I participated in all sports as the seasons came and went and made my letter in basketball in my junior and senior years and track as a senior. Morris and I won the school championship and took second at the state intercollegiate tournament in tennis doubles in our senior year. Morris took first in singles the same year.

*   *   *   *

When I left home that fall it was rather doubtful I would return for Christmas vacation for a number of reasons, most of them having to do with money. But by December 15th even that problem had been eliminated when Dad was able to persuade the railroad management to grant me a trip pass home and back to Helena. I had used Dad's pass on the Milwaukee to Lombard in August but had paid for the rest of the trip on the Northern Pacific from there to Helena.

Although homesickness was never a serious problem for me, there were times when thoughts of home and family were very strong and I was happy that Christmas when the folks decided I should spend the holidays with them. Another important factor was my new baby sister, Phyllis Birdie, whom I had known for only a month before going away to school. She was well worth the trip home.

As usual, Christmas and the following days were happy times for the Midgett family. We had little expectation of numerous and expensive gifts and were usually more than happy with the new clothes and the few toys that made up the bulk of our parents' loving kindness. Of course, the Christmas feast was more than ample for the dozen or more people who gathered around the table including Uncle Jim and Aunt Millie and Aunt Myrtle Fox and her little Bobby.

*   *   *   *

The year of 1921 was critical for Sumatra and the gradually decreasing population of the surrounding area. Most of the faithful few who were still hanging on were confident the weather cycle was due to turn in their favor and another year would bring a revival of the rain, good crops, and the prosperity of the 1910-1917 years in eastern Montana. When the summer season turned out to be almost a carbon copy of 1920, disappointment turned to despair for many families and by spring, 1922 even some of the more strong-hearted had disposed of what was left and sadly joined the ranks of the "departed."

Despite the exodus of the rural population, the little town of Sumatra seemed to weather the storm. Most of the homes continued to be occupied when a few rural families moved into town so their children could go to school. By the early twenties at least half of the small rural schools had closed when most of the district population left the country.

This demise of the rural schools plus the new high school dormitory were two important factors in the prolongation of the life of the town. Following the graduation of high school a single student in 1921, the enrollment increased rapidly and at the end of 1922 a class of nine students received their diplomas. My sister, Elizabeth, was one of the nine and she and two others, Myrtle Smith and Bill Dirrim, followed me to college at Montana Wesleyan that fall. Three more Sumatra graduates, Bernice Rowland, Ray Hoagland, and Jim Bowman also became Wesleyan students in 1923. This was a large delegation of students from a small place like Sumatra.

*   *   *   *

The second trip for the Epworth Leaguers to Institute was scheduled for the week of July 4-11, 1921. The locale of the campground for delegates from our part of the state had been changed to Wolf Creek, about midway between Helena and Great Falls, giving our group an opportunity to see much of Montana new to us. Instead of driving we decided to go by train and our route was, to say the least, a very roundabout one. We left home about nine o'clock on Sunday night on Milwaukee train No. 17 and arrived at Lombard early the next morning after sleeping in our seats for five or six hours. Following a wait of four more hours we transferred to the Northern Pacific, arriving in Helena between 10 and 11 AM after eating breakfast on the train.

When we boarded the train at Lombard the first people we met were Fred Barthelmess and Marjorie Peden, delegates from Miles City, and Esther Wakefield from Forsyth, who were also on their way to Wolf Creek. Fred had also been to school at Wesleyan the previous year so he and I took the rest of the kids on a conducted tour of Helena by street car. Of course, our first objective was the College, then a short trip to the State Capitol, and a quick one out to Broadwater, then the largest indoor warm water pool in the world. A lack of time precluded a swim but some of us would enjoy it many times while college students in Helena.

Since the girls with our delegation had not been to a big town for a long time, they spent the next hour or two window shopping while the boys occupied their time playing pool at the YMCA, where they met Morris Sanford, my roommate, who worked at the Y during the vacation. About 2:30 we all found our way to the Great Northern depot and, after munching a sandwich or two at the lunchroom, we boarded the Butte-Havre train for the ride to our destination. At Wolf Creek station we were met by a bus which, after picking up our luggage, conveyed us about a mile to the campground.

The big meeting tent was located on the west bank of Little Prickly Pear Creek, a beautiful stream rising on the east slope of the Rockies and flowing into Wolf Creek and on into the Missouri River near Holter Dam. The campsite was divided into small plots assigned to each delegation for their tents and campfires. By this time we were a tired bunch and while we boys were pitching our tents, gathering wood, and starting a fire, the female contingent prepared a good nourishing meal of hamburgers and fresh vegetables we had brought from home. We had bought milk at a Wolf Creek store and with coffee it provided the beverage for a meal that tasted like a banquet to a bunch of youngsters who hadn't had a real meal for nearly twenty-four hours.

Arriving at the campground the delegations from Sumatra, Forsyth, and Miles City discovered our lots were adjacent. Fred Barthelmess suggested we combine our initials, S., F., and M.C. and put up a sign designating our quarters as the "ESEFANDEMSEE CAMP." The idea was quickly approved by the rest of us and our banner was the largest one on the entire campground. Although a little puzzled at first, many of the delegates congratulated us on our (Fred's) ingenuity and we were awarded first prize for the most attractive banner.

The program for the week was much the same as at Luccock Park the previous year, except that the recreational activities differed due to the physical features of the surrounding area. Fishing and hiking were popular with the many good streams and challenging mountains only a short distance away. Thursday afternoon at least thirty would-be Izaak Waltons lined up along Wolf Creek for a two-hour fishing marathon with equipment of every description ranging from a tree limb with a string and open safety pin to the latest in rods and reels then available. Prizes were awarded for the biggest fish and for the most fish caught by any one angler. I don't remember who was lucky enough to receive the latter award but one of our boys, Bill Dirrim, hooked a two pound trout and took home a new reel for his performance.

Two other events during the next few days were high spots of the activities at Wolf Creek. The most exciting for me and about a dozen of the other kids occurred Friday afternoon when a scenic trip to Holter Dam and Lake was scheduled. Most of those who had come by automobile drove the ten mile trip but the rest of us signed up to ride the twenty-passenger bus. Upon loading we soon discovered there were too many for the bus so we had to find another means of transportation. This presented a problem until someone thought of the government truck that had been loaned to the convention to haul luggage and equipment from the railroad station to the campground. After due deliberation the trip manager decided to load the remaining kids in the truck if he could find a driver. A young fellow named Pete Gardner from Anaconda and I volunteered to drive if the kids would ride with us.

With a dozen young people loaded on the plank seats along the sides and me behind the wheel for the trip to the dam, everything ran smoothly for the first five or six miles. As we cleared the ridge and started down to the Missouri River and Holter Dam, I tried to reduce gears but couldn't get the transmission from neutral into second gear. Apparently the clutch was not in the best of condition as I could not get the transmission into any gear. I pulled up the emergency brake but nothing happened. Moving downhill, our speed picked up with every yard traveled and I was now dependent entirely on my foot brake. With no air brakes and almost a ton of humanity in the truck the old brake lining was too badly worn to handle the job.

By the time we were halfway down the hill I was a little desperate and I yelled to the riders to hang on. As we approached the last curve before leveling off to the river plain I could see we could not make it without tipping over and tossing people in all directions. There must have been a lot of prayers in that truck for, just as we neared the turn, there in front of us were tracks leading straight ahead through a barbed-wire gate into a cultivated field. The gate was no barrier for the heavy truck and its load and, although the rest of the ride was a little bumpy, we finally came to a halt two or three hundred yards into the field.

We hadn't lost a passenger and the worst anyone suffered were a few superficial bruises, two or three bad scares, and several premature gray hairs for the driver. Needless to say I was very glad it turned out the way it did and was happy to turn the driving over to Pete for the return trip. We took it very easy on the way back and low gear was fast enough for most of us.

The other memorable event of the institute was "Stunt Night" which was held Saturday night on the stage under the big tent where all the general meetings had been conducted during the week. The program had been announced early in the week and every delegation or group was urged to work up an act for the show. Since time for the program was limited, the length of the acts was held to six minutes each plus four minutes to set it up. The first ten groups to register their acts were accepted.

The ESEFANDEMSEE Camp under the direction of Fred Barthelmess, a genius at this sort of thing, put on a skit entitled "The Operation" which really brought the house down. All of us participated in the act as patient, doctors, nurses, medical aides, nurses' aides, and even a janitor who cleaned up the mess after a logging chain, tape measure, a couple of knives, a wrench, a football and a dozen or more small items had been extracted from the patient. He astonished the audience when he made a rapid recovery, jumped off the operating table and ran down the aisle screaming at the top of his voice. The next day at the last general meeting we were awarded the first prize and received a pennant with the words "Wolf Creek Institute, 1921." We gave it to Fred who had made it all possible.

During the week many of the friendships of the previous year were renewed and many new ones developed. I was particularly interested in a couple of cute high school girls from Dillon, Lenora Carney and Francis Brimrose and spent most of my spare time with them. Since I had been at Montana Wesleyan College a year, much of my time was directed toward talking to new high school graduates and directing their interest toward the Helena institution. That fall no less than ten or twelve Instituters enrolled as freshmen at the college including Lenora.

Preparations for our trip home began early Sunday morning. Those of us traveling by train were up and around early taking down our tents and packing our luggage to be trucked down to the station and checked home. The final general meeting of the delegates was held at 11 AM and our train to Helena left about 2:30. We again changed trains there and, after eating our last meal enroute, we left the Capitol City about 8 PM by the NP, arriving at Lombard about 10 PM.

We had a layover there of three or four hours before the Milwaukee Columbian came through. We spent most of the time sleeping in the hard depot seats using our suitcases, coats and other luggage as pillows. A five hour ride through the night brought us home about 8:15 AM. Even though we had tried to sleep most of the time on the train, a tired bunch stumbled down the steps and across the station platform to our cars and home just in time for breakfast.

Chapter XII

The late summer and fall months of 1921 had promised little improvement in the weather situation, but the comparatively few hangers-on in the area were somewhat encouraged when snow began to fall in November. By the first of the year it began to look like old times with two feet of snow on the level and the coulees packed with eight to ten foot drifts where the northwesters dropped their loads after sailing across the flatlands. The chinooks of late February and early March left their marks when little rivulets of snow water merged to form larger and still larger streams rushing into few reservoirs that dotted the countryside. It was a heartening sign and hopes sprang anew in the breasts of the "four score and ten" who still kept the faith.

The change in the general attitude of the people of Sumatra and the surrounding vicinity became very apparent with the coming of spring and another growing season. Not only was there sufficient runoff to fill the water holes but much of the melting snow had soaked into the ground and the natural grasses, dried up for the past three years, turned green again.

Although market prices for wheat and other grain crops had fallen rapidly during the years after the war, supply and demand began to stabilize by 1922 and things looked better for those who had something to sell.

The persistent unchanging faith of the remaining handful of those families who had settled this land between 1910 and 1915 was fully attested in numerous ways in 1922. Not only were there fewer public sales but, to the contrary, a few of those who had abandoned their homesteads when conditions were toughest returned and bought up acreage that they and others had relinquished in 1918, 1919, and 1920. One of the families was the Kelly Kestersons who came back from South Dakota to their place south of town. Thousands of acres taken over by the County for non-payment of taxes were reclaimed and developed into large holdings on which cattle and sheep raising became the principal industries.

Other indications of the renewed faith in the country became evident when the surviving farmers of the area organized the Sumatra Cooperative Shippers Association to more efficiently market their livestock. Officers of the Co-op were Pat Courtney, president; Ray Kock, secretary and M.W. Dorothy, J.A. Smith, Jake Hecker, D.V. Rowland, and Art Weigel, directors. Two years later Art died from tuberculosis, one of the comparative few, other than service men, who passed away during the years the folks lived in Sumatra.

Late in the year the Farmers' Elevator was built to be ready to handle the grain crop anticipated during the summer of 1923. The Sumatra Commercial Club was organized for the purpose of attracting the surrounding population to trade with local merchants. One of its first projects was to dig a well near the Willis Davis place for the convenience of the north country farmers on their trips in and out of town.

The handwriting on the wall so discouraging to so many people during the late teens and early twenties now seemed to hold out the promise of better things for the ensuing years. Instead of giving up and selling out completely, those who remained began looking for some better acreage or added another half section or more to increase their capacity for grain and livestock production. New farming methods were introduced by the State College at Bozeman to conserve available ground water. Production of milk and cream from improved dairy herds showed an increase and "more corn and hogs" became a popular slogan for many of those remaining on their farms.

The generally improved financial condition of the area was reflected in the assets of the local bank which had threatened to close a couple of years earlier when collection of overdue loans became increasingly difficult. Instead of going under, the Sumatra bank, under the management of Bob Ross, fought off the pressures of five years of drought and in 1923 showed assets of nearly $150,000. The local chapter of the Federal Farm Loan Association was reorganized after being defunct for three or four years and money was again made available to farmers who could meet the qualifications. The officers of the newly revived organization were Claude Gray, president, Bill Gutman, vice-president; and Dad was the secretary-treasurer. Dad was one of the first applicants for a loan to plant a wheat crop on our place in the spring 1924 when the folks moved back to the farm.

This was a period of numerous changes in the town's business structure but most were transfers of ownership rather than closings or new ventures. The Jaffe store, which had been sold to M.J. McInaney and E.A. Miller in 1919, changed hands again in 1923 or 1924 when it was purchased by Bill Gutman and Joe Zaharko who renamed it The Economy Supply. A few years later they converted it into a garage. Tom Brown, who had built the implement store and dance hall in 1919, constructed the only concrete block building in town, a garage, on the east side of Main street (one of the few remaining structures still standing on the townsite).

The weekly newspaper, the *Sumatra Record*, published by Ed McRae since 1919, was bought by Uncle Jim Midgett and Joe Cosgrove. The new owners changed the paper's name to the *Sumatra Sun* and the first issue was printed on November 23, 1922. In May 1923 Joe sold his interest to Uncle Jim and bought the store at Hibbard. The paper continued in business until the fall of 1925 when the Jim Midgetts moved to Bridger.

Other changes of ownership occurred during 1922 and 1923 when Dick Imhoff sold his general merchandise store to Claire Ballard and G.A. Over. The Sumatra Mercantile, which had gone into receivership to the Staunton Wholesale Grocery in Roundup, was purchased by Martin Chetkin and renamed the Sumatra Cash Store. The two hotels assumed new proprietors when Mrs. Minnie Herbold sold her "show place" ranch south of town to Bill Youderian and took over the management of the Loraine. Wright Dorothy, who also farmed south of Sumatra, leased his place and moved his family into the Hotel Fleetwood. At least three of his children were ready for high school and the move made it much easier to keep them in school.

Even the one and only saloon and pool hall (by now only a pool hall) seemed to be in some difficulty when Cotton Duff, who had bought it from its original owner, gave it up in 1920. It changed hands three or four more times by 1925. Two of its proprietors for a couple of years each were Clem Kent and Augie Krause, both of whom had been in military service. It was about then that Mrs. Bartlett turned over her garage business to her mechanic, Henry Hayden, and left for her former home in the midwest. Bill Gutman bought out Thad Bassett's dray line and wholesale oil business and the latter moved his family to the Joe Kersner place four or five miles north of town. About the same time Jake Hamre, who had moved his family into town for school, set up a shoe shop in the Economy Supply Store.

Despite apparent indications of some leveling off and possible improvement of general conditions, the area around Sumatra continued to slowly lose its already sparse population. Public sales, although less frequent than in the past three or four years, still occurred at the rate of at least one or two a month.

One obvious effect of this exodus of families a far as Dad was concerned was the gradual decrease in the number of people who needed his medical services and the products available at the drug store. Even the "baby crop" was affected with a decrease in the number of young families in the area and by 1923 Aunt Myrtle, who had operated her maternity home for over five years, found it necessary to take other employment in order to support her little boy and herself. The home was rented in the fall and she took a job as matron and cook at the school dormitory. The following spring she resigned, sold her house, and moved to Missoula where she became house mother for one of the college sororities. Naturally her departure greatly reduced Dad's maternity business.

Yet, the general attitude of the remaining populace of the area was typified by some of the maxims that appeared in advertisements in the weekly newspaper during the years 1922-25. A spirit of optimism was proclaimed: "Our Territory Is Unparalleled For Farming and Dairying;" "Sumatra, Montana-Your Trading Center;" and "A Good Bank In A Good Town."

It was about this time Dad placed an ad in the paper: "Will Sell Only for Cash After January 1, 1924." Nonetheless, I think if anyone needed his services or goods and couldn't dig up the money some arrangement was made to take care of the situation. It is on record, however, that in 1924 he issued a complaint against J.A. Smith for a bill for $160 for goods and services. I believe this was a "first" and probably a "last" for him as his account books showed many hundreds and probably thousands of dollars remaining unpaid not only at Sumatra but other places where he later continued his medical practice.

Despite the departure every week or two during 1922, 1923 and 1924 of another family Dad continued to add a few new babies to the population. News items in the paper announced new arrivals in the families of Joe Barnhard, Frank Burkhart, Peter Burkhart, Dan Finch, Haddon Finch, Jake Grebe, John Hecker, E.C. Kent, Bruce Hayes, Henry Kreider, Bob Seward, Carl Whitney, Matt Reifer, Herbert Wildman, and others. Uncle Jim and Aunt Millie were just as proud as any of these new parents when they announced the adoption of a little girl, Katherine, in January 1922. Then in their mid-forties, earlier efforts to have children had resulted in miscarriages and a stillbirth.

*   *   *   *

The loss of population seemed to have little effect upon the social activities of the community, many of which revolved around the school. The two religious organizations, the Catholic and Methodist churches, continued strong and were well attended by their congregations. A new priest, Father W.J. Charbonneau was appointed to four or five small charges in the area and regular services were held once a month in Sumatra. Rev. W.C. Smith, the Methodist minister at Forsyth, continued his regular monthly visits for almost four years and, in 1923 following his retirement, was replaced by Bertha Reich, a Methodist Deaconess. She was succeeded a year later by Miss Blanche Burton, who preached the baccalaureate sermon for the class of 1925. Father Charbonneau was replaced the same year when he was transferred to a New York diocese.

In spite of "hard times" and the difficulty of raising money to finance their trips, the Epworth Leaguers continued to make their annual pilgrimages to the Institutes every summer from 1922 through 1925. Betty and I were away at school most of those years but returned home for the vacation periods and both of us attended the sessions in

1922 and 1923. Others who were fortunate enough to make the trips were Myrtle and Clara Smith, Bernice, Esther, and Martin Rowland, Ralph and Ray Jones, Lillian and Bessie King, Paul Guthridge, Lloyd Wilson, Mr. and Mrs. Rowland, Miss Bertha Reich, Aunt Myrtle Fox and Reverend Smith.

The 1922 assembly was held at King's Hill campground near Neihart in the Little Belt Mountains, and in 1923 we returned to Luccock Park south of Livingston. Two events of 1922 stick in my memory. It rained nearly all the way to the camp and our Model T I was driving had a flat tire between Harlowton and White Sulphur Springs. The other car, with three girls and Reverend Smith traveling ahead of us, drove right on to the campground, unaware of our trouble. By the time we arrived at White Sulphur Springs it was too late to go further. Night driving on strange roads was seldom done in those days. Ray Jones and I decided to spend the night in our car parked behind the schoolhouse and didn't arrive at the camp until the next afternoon.

For the greater part of the week the weather remained wet and cool, unseasonable for this time in the central Montana summer. Since the camp was located high in the mountains at nearly 7000 feet, we woke a couple of mornings to find an inch or more snow on the ground, a new experience for us from the low range country of eastern Montana.

Most of our leisure time during the week was spent reading and playing indoor games after we had completed the scheduled activities that usually filled most of the morning hours. Saturday was a fun day when the delegates were allowed to go on hikes to the surrounding mines or drive into Neihart and Monarch which, by then, were beginning to look a little like ghost towns.

Saturday night, as usual, was activity night at which the delegates volunteered to participate by presenting some sort of original creation such as a declamation, oratory, one-act play, poem, or other oral production. Participants were given the full week to prepare for their part in the program.

Just how or why I can't recall but some of us delegates from different towns got together and decided to present a debate on the subject of "dancing," which at the time was strictly taboo among devout Methodists. Four of us, two boys and two girls, one of each on a team, agreed on the proposition: "Resolved: That Social Dancing is Harmful to Teenagers," and chose sides by lot. A cute little girl, Ruth Gonser, from Great Falls, and I were paired in the affirmative. I cannot remember our opponents.

There was very little, if any, reference material available on which to base our arguments, so most of our reasoning was founded on our personal ideas and experiences. Since we were all Methodists, bred and raised to accept and conform to the "no dancing" doctrine of the church, Ruth and I felt we had the much stronger case. However, our opponents brought out some very convincing arguments for the negative and the judges voted it a draw. Both teams received many compliments on their presentations and the four of us felt our efforts had been worthwhile.

Although I believe I made my argument persuasively, my sister Betty might not have been convinced. During the previous school year, her senior year in Sumatra, she had slipped out with friends to attend a dance at the school. She escaped an embarrassing confrontation when her companions warned her that Dad, then School Board Chairman, was on his way to oversee the proceedings. It was only much later I learned of this little transgression.

The rain continued to plague us all the way home but, despite slipping and sliding over slick gumbo roads for more than 200 miles, we arrived home late Sunday evening. Crops looked good all along the way and the mood of those people still living in the area was one of high hopes for a good harvest that fall and for the years to come. The natural grasses, which for the past three or four summers had dried up by the middle of July, were still making good growth and farmers were looking forward to a better than average wild hay crop. But such was not to be.

*   *   *   *

In mid-July our expectations of a bumper wheat crop were suddenly dampened when hordes of young grasshoppers hit the fields from above ground and cutworms revealed their destructive presence by attacking the roots of the growing plants. Although the attacks were spotty, those grain fields hit by the insects soon began to show considerable damage.

By the middle of August many fields which in July had been expected to yield 30 to 40 bushels per acre had deteriorated to the point where their owners could hope for no more than half that. Although this was still better than production of the past three years, it was still a big blow to the remaining farm families and a few more were forced to join the exodus.

In spite of continuous population losses, social life among those remaining continued at a pace and the general aspect seemed to be that of restrained cheerfulness—at least in public. Since I was now away at school for nine months of the year, my only contact with our Sumatra friends and neighbors was during the summer. My impression of the popular attitude was that it was a combination of persistent hope and determination to make the best of a consistently bad situation.

There seemed to be no such word or action as "surrender" until every possible solution had bean tried. Sometimes that surrender occurred a little later than it should have. Many people left the country in much worse shape than they might have had they not so stubbornly tried to make something work that was destined only for failure in the end. My parents, sad to say, were one of those families.

Probably the most important single factor affecting the financial condition of the area was the sudden decision of Wiley, Clark and Greening to close the Sumatra Bank and move the assets to Forsyth in February of 1924 after a run by its depositors. Bob Ross was appointed receiver and he promised the remaining depositors he would reopen the bank as soon as possible. He made good on his word and on April 1, 1925, it became the only bank between Forsyth and Roundup. Its new president was Chris Nelson; Bob was reappointed cashier and manager; and H.H. Cloy was the new assistant cashier.

The financial report of the bank on June 30 showed deposits of $138,000, about the same as they had been a year before.

I think it was the closing of the bank that precipitated the move my family made on the first day of May 1924. After selling the big white house in Sumatra to Walt Corcoran they returned to the home on the ranch. Dad had been fortunate enough to keep the place rented every year since the move to Sumatra in 1916, renting on a share-crop basis. But the combination of payments on the ranch and its house, the big house in town and the store building had put him financially behind. His only other source of income was payment for his medical services and supplies and he was never assured of enough from these to pay his expenses on a regular basis. It was indicative of his and my mother's honesty in all their dealings that not only were they able to maintain good credit but in those twelve years from 1914 to 1926 they were never had to face a civil suit for debt.

*   *   *   *

By 1924 I had served my four years and earned sufficient credits to qualify for a B.A. degree in education. I graduated in June with the first class of Intermountain Union College—the new name of Montana Wesleyan when two other denominations joined the Methodists in sponsoring the school in 1923. I had decided during my senior year that I would like to teach and coach athletics in Montana. After applying to a number of schools I was fortunate to be offered a contract with Teton County High School in Choteau where I spent a total of eight years in three separate tenures.

I expected to spend the summer of 1924 at home where I could help Dad run the drug store and test cream as I had the past three years. My plans changed rapidly when in early June, after taking a driver's test late in May, I received a letter from Yellowstone Park requesting me to report by June 17 to drive an eleven-passenger tour bus during the summer season. I had no money, couldn't see how I would get to the Park, and almost wired the company that I couldn't take the job.

That day I walked by a cigar store on Helena's main street and noticed a sign in the window advertising a baseball pool. I had never bet on a pool before but decided on the instant to gamble the last two-bits in my pocket. The clerk in the store told me the winners would be posted next day and I could see whether or not I had won. I followed his advice and imagine my surprise when, on a placard in the window, there was my name with $25 after it. The $25 went for a good cause—the price of a telegram taking the job and a ticket from Helena to the Park on the Northern Pacific. In the end it produced a job as bus driver and agent for the Yellowstone Park Transport Co. for the ensuing eight summers through 1931, a nice arrangement with my summer vacations from the classroom.

My first tenure in Choteau was short-lived. I taught five classes in mathematics and coached football but was dismayed to find that basketball, which I had expected to coach, was to be directed by the principal. After this I sought positions elsewhere in the state and was informed of an opening in the science department and coach of all sports at Sidney High School. I applied and within a few weeks learned the job was mine for the 1925-26 school year. As it turned out the Sidney job lasted no longer, but for a more satisfying reason. The difficulties I had experienced in Choteau had been resolved when the school board fired the principal and wrote asking me to return to my former job, including basketball coaching. So by the time I went home for Christmas holidays, I knew I would be returning to Choteau for a second time.

*   *   *   *

When I went back to Sumatra that Christmas I discovered for the first time that the folks were seriously planning to pull up roots and leave Rosebud County. They wanted to stay in Montana where Dad could continue to offer his medical services to those who needed them.

Conditions in the county had continued to worsen and the area around Sumatra lost more of its few remaining people. The 1924 growing season had started well with favorable amounts of rain through May and June and the early wheat crop had promised 25 to 35 bushels per acre. By July 1 the weather had changed and extremely hot days and nights had begun to shrink the crop. The appearance of dense hoards of young grasshoppers completed the task, stripping many of the fields almost clean. Although much aid was provided by both county and state agencies to fight the insects, most grain crops in the county were too sparse to harvest.

With this recent experience the folks had made their decision. Dad had heard of four or five localities, most of them in the Yellowstone River valley or its tributaries between Miles City and Livingston. While Betty and I were at home during Christmas we made a trip to Huntley irrigation project east of Billings where Dad and Mom were impressed by a couple of locations.

I heard nothing more about their plans to leave until early in February 1926 when a letter from Mom informed me that they had sold the ranch to George Schleder and his sons Bill, Tony, and Ray who lived about a mile and a half southeast of our place. He had sold the drug store to Claude Pickard and they were prepared to move to Bridger, a town of less than a thousand about 30 miles southwest of Billings on the Burlington Railroad. The area had no doctor at the time and it appeared to be a good opportunity for Dad.

For the first time since their arrival in Montana Dad and Mom found themselves rid of the pressures of heavy debt, and the demands of Dad's medical practice kept him busy most of the time. The rest of the remaining family accompanied them; Bob and Olive graduated from high school in Bridger, Olive continuing her education at the University of Montana in Missoula. Betty finished at Intermountain and took a teaching job at Belfry, a few miles south of Bridger. Some years later all, including my parents, would live on the west coast around the Seattle area. I was the only one who remained a Montanan, but I never went back to Sumatra until that day in May in 1970.

EPILOGUE

Requiem For A Ghost

The essential elements for a ghost town were here. Most of the buildings had been either demolished, or moved away. The few surviving structures were vacant and in such a state of deterioration that human habitation was no longer possible. There was one exception, the larger and more distant of the two structures we had seen as we approached the remains of the little town earlier in the morning.

Following our tour of Main Street, which took only a few minutes, our attention returned to the big house on the hill where the Midgett family had lived for eight years. Back on the highway we traveled east a couple of blocks and then south through an open gate to tracks that led to the top of the hill.

As we drove around to the front of the big square eight-room house we saw that although it had lost most of its paint after fifty years of hot summer sun and frigid winter winds, it was still intact and in good condition. Most of the high woven wire fence that had surrounded the house, garden, and out buildings was gone and the yard showed total neglect. Two old car bodies blocked what had once been the street running past the east side of the house.

The gate hung by one hinge on a tipsy rotting post. We walked though it and up to the front stoop. The house appeared to still be somebody's home. Curtains were hung at all the windows and, even before reaching the door, I fully expected someone to open it and greet us with a hearty "hello." As I reached for the screen door, which also hung loosely on rusty hinges, I noticed it was open an inch or two. I knocked and waited. When no one appeared I knocked again. Still no response. My curiosity aroused, I peered through the glass pane. No sign of anyone inside. I turned to Adelaine who was still standing in the yard.

"I can't see anyone in there," I said, "but there are quite a few things scattered around the room and it looks as though someone lives here. I'm going in." Reluctantly, she followed as I pushed the door open and walked into the large living room where my family had spent many a happy hour together. Nostalgia filled my being as my thoughts turned back to my brother and sisters playing or studying by the light of a kerosene lamp and the heat from a big coal stove. I could vividly see my mother finishing the stack of dirty dishes and gently helping the two younger children get ready for bed. I was aware of her gentleness at that moment.

My reverie continued for many seconds before I returned to the present. I realized that something strange had occurred here. Articles of clothing were strewn around the room, and a little red tennis shoe caught my attention. A small child lived here—or had lived here. Two or three pieces of furniture, although upright and undamaged, were in confused disorder, and a general impression was that the room's last occupants had left in a hurry and had never returned.

A small baby-book lying on the entry way to the stairs caught my wife's attention and examining it, we found studio photographs and snapshots of a little girl ranging from an infant to a pretty two-year-old. In other pictures she appeared with other members of the family. The name of the child as well as others were written under each photo but of course they were all unfamiliar to us. An ominous feeling came over me as we looked at the pictures and Adelaine remarked that the discovery of the album assured her that something dreadful had happened in that house. I closed the book and climbed the stairs to the second floor.

A quick survey of the upstairs rooms only amplified our feeling that all was not right in this big old house. Although there were almost no furnishings in the four bedrooms they yielded more of the same kind of evidence we had observed downstairs. Clothing was neatly hung in closets, and numerous small personal objects were where they had been left by the rooms' occupants. Despite the fact that my brother and sisters and I had slept in these bedrooms for quite a few years and I could feel their presence, I didn't stay there long. Now, inexplicably, this was not a pleasant place for me. Although still curious, I was soon ready to leave this place.

We went back downstairs and into the combination kitchen-dining room. There was no table and chairs but many of the usual things to be found in such a room—dishes, eating utensils, pots and pans, even dish towels and articles of clothing—were in their accustomed places. To one side were stacked a number of books—texts or reference books for high school science classes. A name was inscribed in one. I didn't look at the others but my impression was that they might have belonged to a high school teacher, maybe the former resident.

Our inspection of the downstairs complete, we noted that the front bedroom was sealed off from the rest of the house. This, of course, only added to the uneasy feeling about the whole situation into which we had stumbled. Our apprehensions were somewhat assuaged when, back outside, we noticed a sign over a door that had been cut into this room on the north side. In large black letters were the two words "POST OFFICE." The room was empty and apparently had not been used for many months, possibly years.

Adelaine was reminded that she had some post cards she wished to mail to our grandchildren from the town where their granddad lived when he was a boy. After a few more minutes spent wandering around the yard and taking some pictures of the house and its surroundings, we drove back to the highway where we found the post office housed in one-half of a small mobile home. The other half was a small shop where the postmistress sold soft drinks, candy, and other refreshments to tourists who might stop at the lone gas pump in front.

While Adelaine remained outside, I spoke to the young postmistress about the demise of the little town. At that moment my curiosity centered on the big old house and the situation we had just encountered. I introduced myself and explained that I was the son of Dr. Midgett who formerly lived in Sumatra. Since the Midgett era was nearly fifty years earlier the name did not register with her until I mentioned that Dad had built the big house over on the hill.

"Have you been over to the house?" she asked, "I haven't seen anyone around there for quite a few weeks now."

When I replied that we had spent the last half hour looking through the house she indicated considerable surprise.

"Do you mean to tell me that the house was open?" Disbelief was in her voice. "Neither my husband nor I have been over there but other people have told us that the house has been closed up completely for the past several months."

When I told her what we had seen and the riddle it had presented to us as we wandered through the empty rooms empty of human life but full of the evidence of the lively existence of a family, she hesitated a few moments before replying.

"Mr. Midgett, I hesitate to tell you the sad and tragic story of that old house and the family that occupied it," she began. "Actually my husband and I have tried to forget it and have even moved to our present location so we would not constantly be reminded of the terrible experience we went through at that time. But since the episode is an important part of the latter day history of Sumatra and its final demise and is rightly a part of the story you are writing, probably I am in as good, or better, position as anyone to relate the facts to you."

And this is the story she told.

The occupants of the house had been a couple, Phillip and Marie Hauck, and their small daughter, Jean Marie, who had moved there in the late summer of 1967. They had been married for about five years. In his mid-forties the husband was considerably older than his young wife. She was only 24 and had been married shortly after a two-year attendance at college. After their marriage, the couple moved to a farm north of Sumatra which the husband's father had homesteaded nearly fifty years earlier. Although ranching conditions were quite favorable during the sixties and they prospered, their marital relations apparently were not smooth. The older husband was very jealous of his young wife and it wasn't until the birth of the little girl in February 1966, that the conjugal situation showed improvement.

For almost a year the relationship between the two seemed to be quite cordial and marital difficulties, if there were any, were kept well hidden from their friends and relatives. However, by the spring of 1967 the husband's old jealousies had reappeared and, if anything, had grown more intense. Evidences of minor violence against both his wife and baby became apparent and the wife expressed a growing fear of what he might do to her and her child. By early summer she had decided that the only way she could protect her baby and herself was to leave that "madman."

Her threat to leave and take the little girl with her apparently had a conciliatory effect on him. After talking over the situation, the couple agreed on a compromise that they hoped would close the breach between them and restore feelings of respect and concern for each other. They decided to live apart during the week and that he would visit his family on Saturday and Sunday over the balance of the summer and fall seasons. After the fall work on the farm was finished he would move in with them for the winter months and make frequent trips to the ranch to look after the stock.

The problem was to find a place for the wife and her little girl to live. Most of the ranchers and farmers of the homestead period and later had left the country and their homes had either been torn down or, in many cases, moved to other locations. By 1967, with the exception of four or five run-down hovels scattered over the town site, no habitable place still stood in Sumatra except the big house on the hill. Its most recent occupants, the Bernard Yablonsky family, had left the area a few months earlier and the old Midgett residence of fifty years before now stood alone.

In July a deal was completed and the house became the property of the couple who moved in within a few days. At first the arrangement seemed to work out with the husband driving in two or three times a week to be with his family overnight. Friends and relatives were optimistic and hopeful that this solution would turn out to be a happy one for all concerned. During the late summer and early fall of 1967 everything seemed to move along on a fairly even keel with the husband spending most of his time at the farm.

That fall a good crop had been harvested on the few farms still under cultivation in the area. By the middle of October most of the fat stock was on its way to market and ranchers were preparing their places for the long cold winter that could be expected in another month or so. While her husband accompanied a trainload of cattle to the St. Paul market, the young wife and her little girl spent the week with her parents in Forsyth. When he returned to Sumatra she was still away and had left word that she did not intend to return to live with him and had decided to file for divorce.

*   *   *   *

I listened with a certain dread as the postmistress continued her story: "This was the situation on Friday, October 30 as near as it can be determined by those of us who knew them best. Phillip was in town that morning and after picking up his mail and a few groceries at the store he returned to the ranch shortly after noon. What happened later in the day can only be pieced together from the circumstantial evidence found by my husband and a friend of ours who was visiting over the weekend.

"A light snow pushed along by a stiff breeze out of the northwest started falling of Halloween evening. I had been shopping in Melstone and arrived home about dark and had just stopped near our trailer when I noticed the lights of a truck headed toward the big house up on the hill. My children wanted to go over there thinking their little friend, of whom they were very fond, had probably come home from Forsyth. Since dinner was already late and my husband and our guests were half starved, I told the kids to wait until morning. Later I took the kids south of Sumatra to trick-or-treat at a few houses. When we returned the snow was falling and there were no lights on at their house.

"The snow continued through the night and by early Saturday a cold wind had piled up drifts nearly a foot deep. We rose late that morning. We didn't see anyone over on the hill and no smoke coming from the chimney but the Hauck's and their in-laws' trucks were standing in the yard. By noon Saturday the storm had subsided, but there was no activity on the hill. It troubled us somewhat because knowing the difficulties they were having, it was surprising that they had all spent the night together in the house.

"By midmorning of November 2nd the sun had come out and it warmed up considerably. We received a call from another daughter-in-law in Forsyth who was worried about her in-laws. She had expected them home by the night of the 31st. My husband and his friend who had stopped by decided to check on them and started up the hill heading south toward the railroad tracks. As they approached the top of the ridge and looked toward the front of the big house an eerie sight stopped them dead in their tracks. A hundred feet ahead was a pickup truck standing with a door open. It belonged to the folks from Forsyth—the wife's parents—and it was still covered with two or three inches of snow indicating it had been there for at least two days.

"Without approaching any closer the two men continued to examine the scene, now noticing something even more bizarre which fueled their suspicions that something was wrong. Partially covered by snow two bodies were clearly visible between the truck and the house. Backing away from the scene, the men turned and walked rapidly back to the trailer. As they entered the house the pallor of their faces clearly reflected the situation they had just left.

"My husband called Sheriff Andy Shulenberg in Forsyth who arrived with a highway patrolman within a half hour to begin an investigation. The sheriff instructed my husband and the patrolman to cover him from the trailer and beyond, as it was unclear whether anyone might be lying in wait. When he drove up to the house he first thought he saw a curtain move in an upstairs window and dove from his car. It was only then that he caught sight of the husband stretched out dead from a bullet wound that turned out to be self-inflicted.

"By noon the sheriff had called an ambulance that drove up to the front of the house with two attendants and the coroner. Four persons, the young mother and her baby together with her parents, were all dead. The cause of their deaths took more time to establish because of the drifted snow which covered the bodies. It turned out that all four had died of gunshots, that each of the victims had suffered at least one bullet wound. All had apparently been attacked as they stepped down from the pickup truck in which they had ridden from Forsyth. The position of the bodies indicated they had no warning of their danger and no opportunity to escape their killer.

"The young mother's body almost completely covered her child, as if she had tried to protect her. A more thorough examination by the officers after the bodies had been removed to the house revealed that the little one had received a fatal wound from a bullet that had gone through the mother's body.

"After establishing the victims' identities and the extent of the tragedy, two of the officers turned their attention to the body of the husband. The coroner determined that death had resulted from a gunshot wound in the head, self-inflicted by the very unhappy man. The five bodies were placed in the ambulance and taken to Forsyth where the little girl, her mother, and grandparents were buried two days later. The end of the story came with the husband's burial in a Billings cemetery two days later."

She concluded the tale: "They were very nice people. We were becoming friends with the younger couple, especially Marie, and our kids loved Jean Marie. Although we didn't know her parents, we knew of their concern for their daughter and love for their granddaughter. I don't like to think such things can happen."

*   *   *   *

So ended the lives of three of the last meager population of the once thriving little town of Sumatra. And so ended the life of the big white house on the hill which was razed to the ground less than two years after our strange encounter. And so ended the last vestiges of the Midgett contributions to the development of that little town which, fifty years ago, had hopes of becoming a vital and enduring part of the state of Montana. It is only a ghost town now. May it rest in peace.